➤➤➤ Second Edition

CHILDREN'S GAMES FROM AROUND THE WORLD

GLENN KIRCHNER
Simon Fraser University

Allyn and Bacon

Boston ➤ London ➤ Toronto ➤ Sydney ➤ Tokyo ➤ Singapore

To Diane

Vice President: *Paul A. Smith*
Publisher: *Joseph E. Burns*
Editorial Assistant: *Tanja Eise*
Executive Marketing Manager: *Lisa Kimball*
Editorial Production Service: *Chestnut Hill Enterprises, Inc.*
Manufacturing Buyer: *David Repetto*
Cover Administrator: *Jennifer Hart*
Electronic Composition: *Omegatype Typography, Inc.*

Copyright © 2000 by Allyn & Bacon
A Pearson Education Company
160 Gould Street
Needham Heights, MA 02494

Copyright © 1991 by Wm. C. Brown Publishers

Internet: www.abacon.com

Between the time web site information is gathered and published, some sites may
have closed. Also, the transcription of URLs can result in typographical errors. The
publisher would appreciate notification where these occur so that they may be
corrected in subsequent editions.

Library of Congress Cataloging-in-Publication Data

Kirchner, Glenn.
    Children's games from around the world / Glenn Kirchner. — 2nd ed.
       p.   cm.
    Includes bibliographical references (pp.   ) and index.
    ISBN 0-205-29627-0
    1. Games. I. Title.
  GV1203.K65 2000
  796.1'4—dc21   99-41277
                                            CIP

Printed in the United States of America
10 9 8 7 6 5 4 3 2   04 03 02 01 00

Photo credits: Photos courtesy of the author.

►►►

CONTENTS

ABOUT THE AUTHOR

Dr. Glenn Kirchner is an internationally recognized expert in elementary school physical education. His teaching career includes elementary school through university teacher education programs. He has traveled to many countries as an expert clinician and visiting professor. As an author, he has an impressive list of books, manuals, and articles. His textbook, *Physical Education for Elementary School Children,* is now in its tenth edition and is considered a leading text in elementary school physical education. Dr. Kirchner has also produced over thirty instructional films that have been widely distributed throughout the world.

➤➤➤

PREFACE

A few years ago, I started to collect three different types of games from around the world. The first, called *Traditional Games,* are the running, tag, simple ball, guessing, and manipulative games children have played throughout recorded history. The second type, known as *Inventive* or *Creative Games,* are the result of a child's response to a teacher's verbal challenge. In this form of activity, the teacher sets the limitations within which children use their own creative imaginations to make up their own games. The third type, known as *Cooperative Games,* is similar to the second as the teacher sets the limitations relating to such factors as number of players, skills, and equipment to be used. However, in addition to this, these games must also possess one or more cooperative elements, such as cooperation, success, and trust.

Since starting this project, I have received over two thousand games from fifty countries representing six continents. Many of these games were accompanied by photographs of the children playing their traditional and newly created games. In addition, teachers sent collections of drawings made by the children to illustrate how their games were played. More than three hundred of these photographs and children's drawings are included in this edition.

As I edited each game, I tried to keep it as close to the original version as possible. However, there were games in which I had to add a rule, change a sentence, or even change the title to cope with different meanings of words and phrases used in different countries. I also wanted to include as many photographs as possible so that instructors in schools and recreation centers and children from other countries would have a visual idea of where the games came from, what the children looked like, and the type of playing areas they had for their games. The children's drawings provide a pleasant impression of how these young artists felt about their games.

When the participating teachers sent their games to me, they often added a note about the project and how their students reacted to making up their own games. They noticed a positive change in the children's attitude as they began to invent their own games, particularly those of a cooperative nature. This was one of the reasons the teachers gave for planning to use this new approach in their programs. If the reader also believes there is merit in the creative games approach, he or she will be interested in Chapters 7 and 11. These two chapters provide a step-by-step procedure for introducing this approach to young children.

ACKNOWLEDGMENTS

There are many colleagues and friends who provided me with contacts throughout the world. Although I cannot acknowledge all of them by name, they have my thanks for all those introductory letters.

The computer-generated illustrations provided in each chapter were created by Diane M. Smith. Her illustrations not only help clarify the rules and regulations of each game but also capture the fun and excitement of the games.

I would like to give special thanks to my wife for her creative ideas and thorough editing. The following list represents directors of physical education, college teachers, supervisors, and teachers, all of whom gave so generously to this book. To each of them, my sincere appreciation.

Argentina

Professor L. A. Izarduy, Director of National Physical Education and Sports; Mr. M. A. Rezzano, teacher; Mrs. A. L. Virue de Caracciolo, teacher.

Australia

Mr. B. Churchward, Lecturer, Mount Lawley Campus, Western Australia; Mr. F. Wood, teacher; Mr. J. Woodward, teacher; Ms. M. Wincup, Lecturer, School of Physical Education, Underdale Site, South Australia; Mrs. D. A. Monceau, teacher; Ms. D. Peake, teacher; Mrs. J. Best, teacher.

Austria

Doris Kolbl, Magister, Ministry of Education, Strozzigasse, Vienna; Waltraut Hartmann, University of Vienna; Andrea Rieb, teacher; Christa Schubert, teacher; Marliese Pick, teacher.

Bahrain

Ministry of Education, Al Manamah.

Barbados

Ms. A. Brathwaite, teacher; Ms. G. Bailey, teacher; Mr. M. Stoote, teacher; Ms. B. Howard, teacher.

Belgium

Professor R. Renson, Institute of Physical Education, Leuven; Mr. B. Eeclhode, teacher; Mr. C. Schaartz, teacher; Ms. A. Kooreman, teacher; Ms. A. Verreth, teacher; Ms. S. Van Laere, teacher; Professor W. Porte, Hoger Institout Voor Lichamelijke Opvoeding; Dr. D. Van Wouve, Lecturer; Dr. H. Smulders, Lecturer; Dr. B. Vanreusel, Lecturer.

Botswana

Mrs. V. Macdonald, Education Officer, North Kanye; Mrs. M. Mbikiwa, teacher; Mr. L. B. Bogusing, teacher.

Brazil

Dr. J. Carloj Piccoli, Universidale Federal de Pelotas.

Canada

Mr. T. Kikcio, Program Consultant, Saskatoon, Saskatchewan; Mr. D. Bates, teacher; Mr. D. Wipf, teacher; Mr. J. Borland, teacher; Mr. B. McKay, Gabriel Dumont Institute, Regina, Saskatchewan; Mr. G. Smith, Physical Education Supervisor, McCreary, Manitoba; Mr. F. Clark, teacher; Mr. B. Gooden, teacher; Mr. B. Brinksworth, teacher; Mr. F. Hanley, Consultant, Department of Education, Fredericton, New Brunswick; Mr. D. Wilson, teacher; Mrs. D. Tait, teacher; Mr. E. M. Kulmatycki, Coordinator, Red Deer, Alberta; Mr. Stevensen, teacher; Mr. B. Wotherspoon, teacher; Mr. M. Villeneuve, teacher; Mrs. S. Plumber, teacher; Mrs. M. Isenor, teacher; Mr. B. Farnham, teacher; Mrs. Ellen deBruyn, teacher, Surrey, B.C.; Mrs D. De Gagne, teacher; Mr. B. Rosell, teacher, Abbotsford, B.C.

China

Ms. G. Shou, teacher, Shanghai Elementary School, Shanghai, China.

Cuba

Ministry of Education, Havana.

Czech Republic

Dr. F. Mazal, Palacky University of Olomouc; Bela Schneiderova, teacher.

Denmark

Ms. Karen Hoffmann-Jergensen, Skovbyskolen, Skovby, Galten.

England

Mr. C. Cox, Senior Advisor for Physical Education, Chester; Mr. G. Firth, teacher; Mr. J. Oliver, teacher; Mr. C. Pritchard, teacher; Mrs. G. Garnett, teacher; Mr. C. M. Gill, teacher; Mrs. H. Madeley, teacher; Mrs. I. G. Metcalf, teacher; Ms. A. C. Thompson, teacher; Mrs. M. Jameson, teacher; Mrs. P. Cunningham, teacher; Mr. K. N. Jones, teacher.

Estonia

Ministry of Education, Tartu.

France

Madame S. Martine, Institute d'école Primaire Français; Jaunay Clan, teacher; Mr. F. Dart, teacher.

Germany

Professor W. D. Brettschneider, Universität Gesamthochschule, Paderborn; Professor J. Kretchmer, Universität Hamberg; Ms. Hans-Joachim Schnabel, teacher; Professor D. Brodtman, Universität Hannover.

Ghana

Ms. Ama Ashong, teacher; Mr. Damma Huni, teacher; Mr. Timothy Azongo, teacher.

Greece

Mr. P. Konstantinakos, Coordinator, General Secretary of Sport, Athens; Mr. N. Nikitaras, teacher; Mr. Roidis Athanasios, Principal; Mr. Stefanidis Dimitrios, teacher.

Holland

Mr. P. C. Limburg, Director, Research Institute, Arnhem; Ms. T. Steen, teacher; Mr. G. Burken, teacher.

Hong Kong

Mr. Silas Chiang, General Secretary, Hong Kong Sports Association.

Hungary

Dr. G. J. Csaszararne, teacher.

India

Dr. N. Radhakrishnan, University of Baroda; Ms. Swati Jain, teacher; Ms. R. Singh, teacher; Mr. A. H. Goradia, teacher.

Iran

Mr. M. Kashef, Ministry of Education, Karimkhan.

Israel

Mr. Boaz Givon, Director, Recreation and Municipal Department, Jerusalem; Mr. G. Hanita, teacher; Mr. David Monowicz, teacher.

Italy

Dre. E. Ricatti, Ministere Della Publica Instrruzione; Professor A. Berini; Mr. G. Frisa, teacher; Ms. Gividici, teacher; Mr. B. Feltri, teacher; Mr. G. Guidici, teacher.

Jamaica
Ms. K. Simpson, Education Officer, Ministry of Education, Kingston; Mr. D. Smith, teacher; Ms. C. Wilson, teacher.

Japan
Mr. Y. Matsumoto, Instructor, Kyushu Otani College; Mrs. M. Hasegawa, teacher; Mr. Motohiro Skido, teacher; Mr. Endoh Yasuko, Kyoto Kyoiku University.

Korea
Federation of Education, Seoul.

Luxembourg
Mr. R. Decker, Institut Superieur D'Études et de Recherches Pedagogig βéβes; Ms. A. Marc, teacher; Mr. W. Nico, teacher.

Malawi
Mrs. H. Carle, teacher, Mzimba; Mrs. M. Nhlema, teacher.

Mexico
Professor N. R. Rivera Gomez, College General Anaya; Ms. M. Perez Colome, teacher; Ms. A. R. Enriouez, teacher; Ms. D. F. Angeles, teacher.

New Zealand
Ms. J. Silver, Senior Adviser on Physical Education, Department of Education, Auckland; Mr. K. Hornby, teacher; Mr. D. Douche, teacher; Ms. R. Denly, teacher.

Nigeria
Dr. M. O. Ukah, College of Education, Benure State University; Mrs. M. Tondo, teacher; Mrs. F. Ihekuna, teacher.

Peru
Professors L. Matos and F. Temoche, Universidad Nacional de Trujillo; Mr. R. Segura, General Director, Continuing Education; Mr. F. N. Rodriguez, Director, Physical Education and Sports.

Poland
Dr. Cezary Droszcz, University Komitet do Spraw Mlodziezy, Warszawa; Ms. E. Kardas, teacher.

Romania
Mr. A. Anghelesw, Ministry of Education, Bucuresti; Mr. B. Nicolai, teacher.

Russia
Mr. V. Motopin, Teacher Training College, Min-Vody.

Saudia Arabia
Ministry of Education, Riyadh.

Scotland
Mrs. I. R. Drummond, Head Teacher, Helensburgh, Dunhartonshire; Ms. J. Howie, teacher.

Singapore
Mr. J. Scurlar, College of Education, Singapore.

South Africa
Mrs. J. E. Du Toit, Lecturer, Department of Physical Education, Universiteit Van Stellenbosch; Ms. J. A. Skibbe, teacher; Mrs. M. C. Grant, teacher; Ms. L. Hutcheson, teacher; Ms. L. Rbeeder, teacher; Mrs. M. Levvennick, teacher.

Spain
Mr. J. C. Oliva, Plaja de Astilluo, Madrid.

Sweden
Mr. S. T. Andersson, Lecturer, Stockholm Institute of Education; Mr. B. Lundquist, teacher; Mr. K. van Malmburg, teacher.

Switzerland
Dr. F. Wettstein, Pro Juventute, Zurich; Ms. K. Rentsch, teacher.

Syria
Mr. M. Schaher Schwekain, Ministry of Education, Damas.

Thailand
Mr. S. Puangbootr, Director General, Department of Physical Education, National Stadium, Bangkok, Thailand.

United States of America
Mrs. M. Reimer, teacher; Ms. D. Long, teacher; Ms. N. Hovde, teacher; Mr. R. Metz, teacher; Mr. G. Brown, teacher; Ms. L. Vitaglione, teacher; Mr. R. Rhatigan, teacher; Mr. R. Marston, Professor, University of Northern Iowa; Mr. V. Else, teacher; Ms. K. Needham, teacher; Ms. J. Barnes, teacher; Ms. N. Schreiber, teacher.

Wales
Mrs. A. Lyons, teacher, St. Clare's Convent Prep School, Porthcawl, Mid Glam, South Wales.

Zimbabwe
Ms. M. Collen, Singwangombe Primary School, Nkayi; Ms. E. Musangeya, teacher.

INTRODUCTION

In 1823 Alfonso X, the Spanish king of Castile, compiled one of the first game books in recorded history. Since then many other books have been written about the various types of games played by children, youth, and adults. Some of these publications, such as Joseph Strutt's *Sports and Pastimes of the People of England*, written in 1898, and Edward and Elizabeth Lucas's book, *Three Hundred Games and Pastimes*, published in 1900, are collections of games with historical background about how, why, and where the games were played. Contemporary books on this topic often provide theories as to why children play particular types of games along with descriptions of games played in various parts of the world.

This book, a result of a collaborative project conducted with hundreds of elementary school teachers from fifty participating countries, is different from the above publications in that, as well as traditional games, it also includes new games that the children have discovered for themselves. In Part One, the traditional games that have been played for centuries are described and illustrated. Many of these games are also accompanied by photographs and drawings that were done by the children themselves.

Part Two contains a variety of new games that were created by children. These games were arrived at through a process in which their teachers posed special challenges that required one or more players to make up games using a variety of inexpensive equipment such as balls, sticks, and other small objects. A selection of the games in this part of the book is also accompanied by children's drawings or by photographs.

Part Three is an extension of the new games section. It contains cooperative games designed by the children using the same process of posing special challenges with an important criterion added: Each challenge in Part Three required the game to include one or more elements of cooperative behavior. These elements were defined as cooperation, fun, equality, participation, success, and trust. Like the two previous sections, the new games in this section are generously illustrated with drawings and photographs.

The initial intent of this book was to provide a reservoir of old and new games for the participating teachers to share. The traditional games of Part One clearly illustrate the common purpose games had in the past and will continue to have in the future for children of all ages regardless of their cultural backgrounds. Hopefully, the new games in Parts Two and Three will be played by other children and added to their own reservoir of enjoyable games, thus fulfilling the wish of the teachers and children who participated in this project that their contributions, particularly those games of a cooperative nature, will provide a closer bond of understanding and friendship among nations.

►►►Part One

POPULAR TRADITIONAL GAMES FROM SIX CONTINENTS

Chapter One: Running and Tag Games
Chapter Two: Simple Ball Games
Chapter Three: Manipulative and Guessing Games

Part One contains over one hundred traditional games played by children in every part of the world. These are not the highly organized sports like basketball and soccer; rather, they are the uncomplicated games that require little equipment and are played in the streets, vacant lots, or parks by city children and in the open fields and forests by country children. They include running games, which generally involve one or more taggers, boundaries, and special rules. They also include simple ball, guessing, and manipulative games like marbles, hopscotch, and rock, scissors, paper.

One of the most interesting features of these traditional games is that they are all, with one or two exceptions, competitive in nature. A single player either competes against another player, as in hopscotch or marbles, or as part of a team against another group. Children are either tagged, caught, or in some way eliminated from the game until a winner is declared. Another interesting discovery was that teachers and children from various parts of the world believed their games, be it "Esha Desai," "Prisoner's Base," or "Drop the Hanky," were unique to their country. They did not realize their games were played by other children from different cultural backgrounds and geographical locations around the world. With few exceptions, what we find is quite the contrary; the various types of traditional games, described and illustrated in Part One, are the universal language of children. These games, as you will soon read, may have different names and slight variations in the rules, but they are played by children of all ages and in most countries of the world. The games provided in the next three chapters are examples of these "universal" games along with a few truly unique games from each participating country.

The origin of many of the games described in the next three chapters goes back hundreds, and, at times, thousands of years. A few historical notes are provided for some of them to give the reader and, hopefully, the children who play them, an idea of how and why children have always played these games. As adults, we have presented a number of theories as to why children have always played games. For the young player, the rationale may not go beyond one very important reason—to enjoy the excitement of the game.

➤➤➤Chapter One

RUNNING AND TAG GAMES

The games included in this chapter are perhaps the oldest and most well-known games played by children in every country of the world. Many of these games date back to early Egyptian, Chinese, and Pre-Christian civilizations. For example, in early Greek times, a game called "Brazen Fly" was played in almost the same way as "Blindman's Bluff," and hopscotch diagrams have been found on ancient Roman tiles that are similar to those played by children on today's streets and playgrounds on every continent. During the reign of the English king Edward III (1327–77), "Prisoner's Base" was banned from the grounds of Westminster Palace because it interfered with parliamentary affairs. As you will soon read, the game is still played in much the same way as in King Edward's time, and, of course, is no longer banned by teachers or recreation leaders. Other games, such as "Red Rover," "Drop the Hanky," and "Stuck in the Mud," can be traced back to early Greek and Roman times. Historical records in such countries as Iran, India, Japan, and Greece include references to many of the running and tag games described in this chapter.

The games that are included in this chapter normally involve seeking and chasing, dodging, and especially tagging another player.

➤➤TAIL OF THE RAT

Country: Switzerland
Type: Running and Tag
Players: 16 or more
Age: 9–12
Equipment: Tape recorder

➤➤HOW TO PLAY

The game begins with the players scattered in the playing area. Everyone closes their eyes while

FIGURE 1.1   . . . begins to perform

the leader moves through the area and silently touches one of the players to become the Rat. On signal, everyone opens their eyes and begins to move to the rhythm of the music. Suddenly, the Rat begins to perform a special movement, such as jumping with both hands held overhead. As the Rat continues to perform this movement, other players who detect she is the rat, run behind her and mimic her movements. When the Rat has six or more players behind her, she stops, spread her legs, and every player in line must follow her movements. All other players must crawl through the legs. The game starts over with the leader finding a new Rat.

FIGURE 1.2   . . . must crawl through . . .

FIGURE 1.3   . . . the rabbit stands in the . . .

▶▶RABBIT IN THE HOLE

Country: Peru
Type: Tag
Players: 16 or more
Age: 6–8
Equipment: None

FIGURE 1.4   . . . rabbit to its hole

Name of Game	Country	Type	Players	Age	Equipment	Page
Tail of the Rat	Switzerland	Run & Tag	16 or more	9–12	Tape recorder	3
Rabbit in the Hole	Peru	Tag	16 or more	6–8	None	4
Kick the Can	Canada	Run & Tag	16 or more	8–12	Tin can	6
Black Cat	Germany	Run & Tag	16 or more	8–10	Ropes	8
Snow White	Australia	Run & Tag	16 or more	7–12	Hoops	8
Running Steps	South Africa	Tag	6–20	9–12	Stairs	9
Tradhok	Sweden	Run	16 or more	7–12	Tree	10
Dog and Bone	Barbados	Run & Tag	10–20	7–12	Stick	10
Fire on the Mountain	Nigeria	Run	16 or more	6–8	None	11
Stuck in the Mud	England	Run & Tag	16 or more	7–12	None	12
Cat and Rat	Barbados	Run & Tag	10–12	6–8	None	14
Somersault	Greece	Run	16 or more	9–12	Rope	14
Red Rover	U.S.A.	Run & Tag	16 or more	7–12	None	15
Eagle Eats	Zimbabwe	Tag	10–12	6–8	None	16
Ice Cream	Wales	Run	16 or more	6–8	None	17
Drop the Hanky	China	Run	16 or more	6–9	Cloth	18
Stinger	South Africa	Run & Tag	16 or more	8–12	Ball	20
Lemon, Lemon	Belgium	Run	16 or more	8–12	Ball	20
Prisoner's Base	England	Run & Tag	16 or more	8–12	None	21
Emergency	Canada	Run & Tag	16 or more	8–12	None	22
Step on My Shadow	Botswana	Run & Tag	16 or more	8–10	None	23
Alley Cat	Japan	Run & Tag	16 or more	8–12	None	23
Divisible Snakes	Luxembourg	Run & Tag	16 or more	8–12	None	24
Mic Mac Relay	France	Run	16 or more	9–12	None	24
Carbonales	Peru	Run	16 or more	8–12	None	25
KHO	India	Run & Tag	16 or more	8–12	None	26
Electric Gate	China	Run & Tag	16 or more	9–12	None	26
Five-and-Ten Ball	Belgium	Run & Tag	10–16	9–12	Bag	27
Number Relay	Brazil	Run	16 or more	9–12	Beanbag	27
Laobat A-Haloo	Bahrain	Ball & Tag	5–7	8–12	Ball	28
Eyeglasses	Korea	Run & Tag	16 or more	7–10	None	28
Open the Window	Denmark	Run & Tag	7	9–12	None	29
Crazy Circle	Spain	Tag	8–10	9–12	None	29
Chick Chickabiddy	Estonia	Run & Tag	6–8	6–9	Small object	29
Carriage and Driver	Greece	Run & Tag	16 or more	9–12	None	30
Lion in the Den	Nigeria	Run & Tag	16 or more	6–10	None	30
Wall Refuge	Singapore	Run & Tag	6–10	9–12	None	30
Sugar and Honey	Ghana	Run	16 or more	6–9	None	31
Omlar	Iran	Run & Tag	16 or more	9–12	None	31
Crosscut Beancurd	Hong Kong	Run & Tag	5	7–9	None	32
Snake Bridges to Sea	Mexico	Tag	16 or more	9–12	None	32
Chase in Order	Saudi Arabia	Run & Tag	10–20	8–12	None	34
One, Two, Three	Switzerland	Run & Tag	16 or more	9–12	None	34
Add a Movement	Syria	Run & Tag	16 or more	7–10	None	35

▶▶HOW TO PLAY

The players are arranged into groups of three and scattered in the playing area. Within each group two players join hands to form a hollow tree and the third player, the Rabbit, stands in the middle. One of the groups is designated as extra Rabbits that then separate and find their own individual places in the playing area. When the teacher calls, "Rabbit to its hole!" the two players forming the hole raise their arms to let out the Rabbit who, in turn, must run and find a new hole. The extra Rabbits also run to any open hole, but only one Rabbit is allowed per hole. The game continues, changing positions between the hole players and the Rabbits, until all players have had a chance to be a Rabbit.

Note: This game is also played in Australia, Canada, United States, and England usually by the name Squirrel in the Tree.

►►KICK THE CAN

FIGURE 1.5   . . . if the player gets to . . .

Country: Canada
Type: Run and Tag
Players: 16 or more
Age: 8–12
Equipment: 1 tin can

The origin of Kick the Can appears to be about the middle of the last century in Great Britain. It was called various names, such as "Kick Can Bobby," "Kick Can Copper," and "Kick the Block." The latter name was used because children kicked a wooden block or stone. When the tin can became available, it was easier on the foot and produced more noise, to the enjoyment of the players and to the annoyance of the neighborhood. There are numerous references to this game in contemporary games books. The number of variations described below attest to the popularity of this game around the world.

►►HOW TO PLAY

One player is chosen to be It and stands in a circle next to a tin can. When It closes her eyes and begins to count aloud to fifty, all other players run and hide. After It counts to fifty, she begins to look for hidden players. When she finds a player, they both run for the tin can. If It tags the can first, she says "one, two, three" and the name of the player, then that player goes to a designated Jail. However, if the player gets to the can first, he/she kicks the can as far as possible to release any player(s) in jail. It must replace the can and count to fifty before she starts looking for hidden players again. The game continues until all players are caught or It is changed after a set period of time.

►►VARIATIONS

►India: Esha Desai (I Spy)

In India, the game is played in a similar fashion except, to start the game, any player picks up the tin can and throws it under her leg as far as possible. Once It returns the can to the circle, all she has to do is visually "spot" a player who becomes the new It.

►Holland: Burkuit (Kick the Can)

A favorite street game and played exactly the same as the Canadian version—except children hide in and around buildings.

►Sweden: Paven Bannlyser (The Pope)

In Sweden, the Pope stands on a small hill, and counts to 100 while others run and hide. The Pope then goes to find the children. When a child is seen, the Pope says: "Peter (the player's name), you are banished." Peter must walk to the Pope's hill and wait until he receives a "wave" (signal) from one of the hidden children. When Peter has been waved free in this way, he must sneak away without being seen by the Pope. If the Pope sees Peter or any other player sneaking away, he or she is banished again. The game continues until a player is banished three times. When this occurs, all players come out of hiding and the game begins again with a new Pope.

►Japan: Kankai

The group is divided into Taggers and Runners. One runner kicks the can out of the circle. As soon as any player on the Taggers' team returns the can to the circle, all taggers try to tag the runners. When a runner is touched, he must stand in the

FIGURE 1.6   . . . and counts 1, 2, 3, 4 . . .

circle. However, like the other versions, if a runner can kick the can without being touched, he releases all other runners.

➤ Switzerland: Shiiti (Knock over the Logs)

Three sticks in the form of a triangle are placed in the middle of the playing area. A small square is drawn near the pyramids to be used as a goal. One player is

FIGURE 1.7   . . . to run and hide . . .

chosen to be the Warden. All other players run and hide in the surrounding area. On a signal from the teacher the "Warden" carefully moves away from the pyramid and tries to find other players. As soon as the Warden finds a player, he/she runs back and touches the pyramid and calls out the player's name. The player must run to the jail and remain there until freed by a teammate.

►Cuba: Hide and Throw the Tin Can

This game is played in the same way as the Canadian version, with one exception. One child is chosen to be the Whistle and another child, the Counter, stands behind him and both players face away from the playing area. To start the game, the Whistle blows his whistle, signaling the Counter to begin counting up to fifty and for all other players to run and hide. The pace at which the Counter counts determines how much time the players have to run and hide.

►►BLACK CAT

Country: Germany
Type: Tag
Players: 16 or more
Age: 8–10
Equipment: Set of skipping ropes

►►HOW TO PLAY

One player, the Black Cat, stands on the side of the playing field. The other players, Mice, stand on the opposite side. Each Mouse has a tail (skipping rope tucked into back of shorts). The Black Cat calls, "Who's afraid of the Black Cat?" The Mice reply, "Nobody!" The Black Cat says, "I'm coming!" The Mice try to run to the opposite side without allowing the Cat to step on their tails. When a Mouse loses his tail, he becomes the Black Cat and the game starts over.

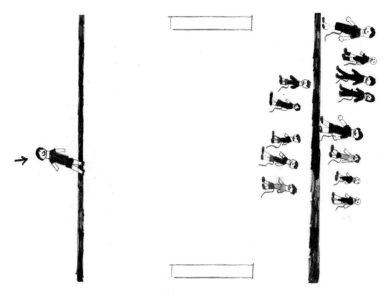

FIGURE 1.8   . . . Who's afraid of the black cat . . .

►►SNOW WHITE

Country: Australia
Type: Tag
Players: 16 or more

Age: 7–12
Equipment: 8 hoops and
2 cones

▶▶HOW TO PLAY

The children are divided
into seven teams. Each
team chooses a name of
one of the Seven Dwarfs,
such as Happy, Dopey,
or Doc. One child is se-
lected to be the Witch
(tagger), another child
becomes Snow White
and stands in the single

FIGURE 1.9   . . . Children who are tagged . . .

hoop as shown in the illustration. All teams line up behind a home line with the
Witch standing anywhere within the playing area (suitable for indoors as well as
outdoors). The Witch calls a name such as Grumpies and they try to run to the
opposite line and back before being tagged by the Witch. The only safe area is
behind the home line. Children who are tagged are sent to the Dungeon (hoops)
where they wait to be freed by Snow White, who can, at any time, sneak across
and touch them to set them free. This is a very heroic gesture on Snow White's
part as she runs the risk of being tagged by the Witch. If this happens, Snow White
is replaced by another child. The game ends when all groups have had a turn at
running down and past the Witch. A new Witch is chosen to start the next game.

▶▶RUNNING STEPS

Country: South Africa
Type: Tag
Players: 6–20
Age: 9–12
Equipment: Stairs

FIGURE 1.10   Aar Speler

FIGURE 1.11   . . . At the bottom of the stairs . . .

▶▶HOW TO PLAY

The game can be modified according to the number of steps that are available. Each step is assigned a day of the week. The Caller stands on the flat surface at the bottom of the stairs (Saturday) and calls out the name of a day. The players stand on the neutral area at the top of the stairs and must move to the step that was called out. If they move to the wrong step, they are eliminated. If the Caller says "Saturday!", all the players must touch the bottom area with one foot, then run back to the neutral area. The Caller tries to tag a player as soon as she touches Saturday. However, the Caller is not permitted to climb the stairs in pursuit of the players. If a player is tagged, she becomes the new Caller.

▶▶TRADHOK (TREEHAWK)

Country: Sweden
Type: Run and Tag
Players: 16 or more
Age: 7–12
Equipment: Trees, traffic cones, or beanbags

FIGURE 1.12   . . . The hawk must find a . . .

▶▶HOW TO PLAY

One player is chosen to be the Hawk. All other players must find a Tree (any designated spot) and touch it. The object of the game is for any two players to signal to each other by blinking their eyes then running to each other's tree. The Hawk must find a free tree before any set of players can complete their exchange. If the Hawk is successful, the player who did not reach his tree becomes the new Hawk and must call out "I am the new Hawk," and the game continues.

▶▶DOG AND BONE (STEAL THE BACON)

Country: Barbados
Type: Run and Tag
Players: 10–20
Age: 7–12
Equipment: A small item, such as a stick or beanbag

FIGURE 1.13   . . . When a player

▶▶HOW TO PLAY

Two teams line up behind their own end lines. Each player has a number and the beanbag is placed in the middle of the playing area. The teacher calls out a number, such as four, and the fours from each team race for the Bone. When a player picks up the Bone, he must run back across his own end line without being tagged by the opposing number four player. If touched by the opposing player before reaching his end line, his opponent receives one point. On the other hand, if the player reaches his end line without being tagged, his team is awarded one point.

▶▶VARIATIONS

▶Belgium: Tie Robbery

Played exactly the same way except that they use a cloth for the Bone and call it a Tie.

▶India: Dog and Bone

This game is played as it is in Barbados and Belgium, with one exception. When a number is called, a player must pick up the Bone within a specified time—say, ten to fifteen seconds. If neither team picks up the Bone, they return to their own lines and another number is called.

▶Peru: Struggling Flags

This game is very similar to Dog and Bone but with a nice variation. Two teams are numbered and stand on a line facing the teacher who is holding a flag in each hand. The teacher calls a number, such as five, then two players, one from each team, race for their flag, run around their own team, return the flag, and run back to their starting positions. The player who returns to his own place first wins one point for his team.

▶▶FIRE ON THE MOUNTAIN

Country: Nigeria
Type: Running
Players: 16 or more players
Age: 6–9
Equipment: None

FIGURE 1.14   . . . runs as fast as . . .

▶▶HOW TO PLAY

One player is selected to be the leader. The rest of the children get into pairs and form a large circle with one partner (partner A) in front of the other (partner B) and all facing clockwise. The leader stands in the center of the circle. When he calls out "Fire on the mountain," everyone begins to run slowly in a clockwise direction, chanting "run, run, run." As the children are running, all player B's begin to speed up to pass their partners on the outside of the circle, and keep running as fast as they can. When the leader calls out, "Fire is out," all player A's run as fast as they can, continuing in the clockwise direction, to catch up to their partners. The last set of partners to meet go to the center of the circle. All remaining players change positions (that is, player A becomes player B and vice versa) and the game is repeated. The last remaining pair is declared to be the winner.

▶▶VARIATIONS

▶Malawi: Moto Kumapiri (Fire on the Mountain)

One child is chosen to be It and the remainder of the class is divided into two groups of the same number. They then form a double circle and face counterclockwise with It standing outside the circle, also facing counterclockwise. It begins to run around the circle and sings "Moto kumapiri, moto kumapiri." All players join in singing "Moto . . . , moto . . . ," and both circles begin to run counterclockwise. Suddenly It calls "Wazima!," which means the fire is out. When this happens, It and all the children on the outside circle try to find and hold onto a

FIGURE 1.15   . . . It calls . . .

player on the inside circle. The player who remains alone becomes the new It and the game starts over.

▶▶STUCK IN THE MUD

Country: England
Type: Run and Tag
Players: 16 or more
Age: 7–12
Equipment: None

▶▶HOW TO PLAY

Two or three players are chosen to be Taggers with the rest of the class scattered in the playing area. Taggers try to tag the other players. When

FIGURE 1.16   . . . When an untagged player . . .

a player is tagged, she must stand with legs apart. When an untagged player crawls under the tagged player's legs, she is freed and can join the game again. However, if a player is caught three times, she becomes one of the Taggers. If the turnover is not frequent enough, change Taggers every few minutes.

▶▶VARIATIONS

▶Germany: Bridge Tag
Same rules.

▶United States: Smurf Tag
This version is similar to Stuck in the Mud with a few space-age additions. The Taggers are known as Gargomels and are identified by wearing colored pinnies and carrying a Nerf ball. All other players are Smurfs. When a Smurf is tagged, he must freeze with hands held high and legs apart. He may be released when another Smurf crawls through his legs. However, if a Smurf is tagged while in the act of crawling through another Smurf's legs, he must stand in front of the would-be-liberated Smurf with legs apart and hands held high. Both captured Smurfs can only be released if another Smurf crawls through both players' legs.

➤Romania: Smile and You're It

This game is similar to Stuck in the Mud, except that, just before a player is touched, he may stop and become a motionless statue. The Tagger then tries to make the Statue move or laugh without touching him. If the Statue laughs or moves any part of his body, he changes places with the Tagger and the game continues.

➤Denmark: Mat Catching Tag

All players move on two small mats. One player is chosen to be It. The game is played as regular tag except that, if a player loses his balance and falls off one or both mats, he changes places with the Tagger. When a player is caught, he must bend down and "freeze" to the ice. Any player who is caught may be rescued by having two other players join hands and make a Bridge over him.

➤Czechoslovakia: Rabbit Chase Tag

One player is chosen to be the Fox and all other players are Rabbits. All Rabbits, except one, scatter around the playing area and sit down. On a signal, the Fox begins to chase the Rabbit. The Rabbit can, at any moment, save himself by sitting

FIGURE 1.17   . . . must get up and run away . . .

FIGURE 1.18   . . . by sitting down . . .

down beside another player. As soon as this happens, the Rabbit that sits beside must get up and run away from the Fox. If the Fox catches the Rabbit, they change positions and the game continues. A second Fox can be added to the game to increase excitement and participation.

▶▶CAT AND RAT

Country: Barbados
Type: Run and Tag
Players: 10–12
Age: 6–8
Equipment: None

▶▶HOW TO PLAY

One player is chosen to be the Rat and stands in the middle of the circle. Another player is the Cat and stands outside the circle, which is made up of the remaining players. Circle players hold hands while Cat and Rat act out the following challenge:

> Cat: "I am the Cat."
> Rat: "I am the Rat."
> Cat: "I can catch you!"
> Rat: "No, you can't!"

This chasing game begins after the word *can't*. Rat and Cat may move in and out of the circle by crawling under the joined hands of the circle players. As soon as the Cat touches the Rat, two new players are chosen and the game continues.

▶▶VARIATIONS

▶Canada

Same name, same game.

▶United States: "Cat and Mouse"

Circle players join hands and try to prevent the Cat from catching the Mouse by moving their arms up and down.

▶▶SOMERSAULT

Country: Greece
Type: Running
Players: 16 or more
Age: 9–12
Equipment: Long rope

▶▶HOW TO PLAY

Arrange two teams as shown in the diagram. Children in group A form a circle and hold on to the rope with both hands. One player (Leader) of group A holds one end

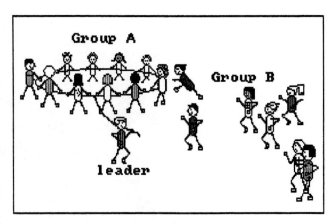

FIGURE 1.19   . . . holds one end . . .

of the rope. Players from group B try to jump on the backs of group A. The Leader of group A is allowed to move around the circle while holding the end of the rope, to try and stop group B players from climbing onto the backs of his teammates. The Leader of group A cannot use his hands, . . . only the rope or his body to hinder the Attacker. If a player successfully climbs onto a group A player's back, the A player must carry him to a designated line. Player A remains behind the line and Player B returns to the game. The aim is for players from group B to climb onto the back of each player in group A, thus eliminating them from the game. To repeat the game, all players rotate position.

➤➤RED ROVER

Country: United States
Type: Run and Tag
Players: 16 or more
Age: 7–12
Equipment: None

Although this game has been played in many countries for at least the past two hundred years, its exact origin is still unknown. One of the first references was in 1898 to a Scottish game called "Jockie Rover," which had a Chaser and a Den. Before the Chaser came out, he called out "Jockie Rover, three times over, I'll gie you a blover." The game was played in Brooklyn around 1890 under the title "Red Lion," and with the following challenge:

> Red Lion, Red Lion,
> Come out of your den,
> Whoever you catch
> Will be one of your men.

➤➤HOW TO PLAY

One player is chosen to be the Tagger and stands halfway between the goal line and another line at the opposite end of the playing area. All other players stand behind one goal line. The game starts when the Tagger calls, "Red Rover, if you don't come I'll pull away!" After this call, all of the players try to run across to the opposite goal without being tagged. All of those tagged join the Tagger and help to tag the rest when the original Tagger gives the call again. The game continues until all players are caught. The last one caught becomes the Tagger for the next game.

This game can be played with the following variation: After the Tagger has caught four to five players, the runners on the goal line have two choices. They may continue to try to run to safety or they may stay behind the line to "tug." To "tug," the people on the goal line call out, "Tug!" and then take the first hand offered them by one of the Taggers. If the person on the goal line can pull the tagged person over the line, she has a free run to the other line. If the person on the goal line is pulled over by the tagged player, he becomes a tagged player.

➤➤VARIATIONS

➤England: British Bulldog
Instead of each player being tagged, It has to catch a Runner and hold him off the ground while he says, "British Bulldog one-two-three." If the Tagger can hold the player off the ground for three counts, that player becomes another Tagger. If the Tagger cannot hold the Runner off the ground for the required count, the runner is freed and continues to run to the opposite line.
➤South Africa: Open Gates
Same rules as the United States.

FIGURE 1.20   Open Gates

➤ New Zealand: Bull Rush

The game begins with It calling out the name of one player who must then run the length of the playing area without being tagged. If the Runner is caught, he helps the Tagger and another player is called to run. If the Runner is successful in reaching the goal line, all other players have a free run to the opposite line. The game continues until every player is tagged.

➤ Canada: Pom Pom Pull Away

Same rules as the United States. As well as an indoor game, this game is also played in rural areas on skates on outdoor rinks where the call is, "Pom Pom Pull Away. If you don't come, we'll drag you away!"

➤ Octopus

In this other Canadian variation of the traditional game, two or three players are chosen to be It. The remaining players line up on the end of the playing area. To begin, the Its yell "Octopus!" This signals the players to try to run to the opposite safety zone without being tagged. Any tagged players must stand at the spot where they were tagged. Again, when the Its yell "Octopus!", the untagged players try to move to the opposite safety zone. This time, however, the runners must be more wary because in addition to the mobile taggers, the "frozen" tagged players may pivot on the spot and tag them. The game continues until there are two or three players remaining untagged. These players become the Its for the next game.

➤ Greece: Rabbit and Hunters

Same rules as the United States.

➤➤ THE EAGLE EATS

Country: Zimbabwe
Type: Tag
Players: 10–12
Age: 6–8
Equipment: None

➤➤ HOW TO PLAY

One player is chosen to be the Old Eagle, another is the Chicken, and the remaining players are Chicks. The Chicks hold onto each other's waists and hide behind the mother Chicken, who tries to keep between the Old Eagle and her Chicks. The

FIGURE 1.21 . . . tries to tag . . .

Old Eagle tries to tag any Chick. When a Chick is caught, he must sit down on the side and wait until the last Chick is caught.

➤➤VARIATIONS

➤China: Old Eagle
Same rules as Zimbabwe.

➤➤ICE CREAM (RED LIGHT)

Country: Wales
Type: Running
Players: 16 or more
Age: 6–8
Equipment: None

This is probably best known as "Red Light" and its origin is probably somewhere in Europe around the middle of the nineteenth century. When the first electric lights blinked red and green in New York around 1919, a new name, "Red Light Green Light," was given to this game. As the years passed, it has become known as "Red Light." Although it is played in many countries, the name may change but the rules are similar.

FIGURE 1.22 . . . she quickly turns . . .

➤➤HOW TO PLAY

One player is chosen to be It and faces the wall. All other players stand on a line about thirty feet away. It begins to spell aloud, "I-C-E-C-R-E-A-M." When she finishes spelling the word, she quickly turns around to catch anyone moving forward. When a player is caught, she must stand next to It and place one hand on the wall while all other players return to the starting line. The game starts again, and if anyone can get to the wall before It finishes spelling the word, the caught players are freed and all runners head back to the starting line. It runs after them and, if she tags one, that player becomes the new It. If not, she remains It and the game continues.

➤➤VARIATIONS

FIGURE 1.23 Same rules, different name . . .

➤Canada: Red Light
Same rules, same game.
➤Japan: Druma
Same rules, different name.
➤Switzerland: Ice Cream
Same rules, same name.
➤Jamaica: Red Light
Same game except that It counts from one to ten, and says Red Light before turning around to catch the players who are still moving.
➤United States: Red Light
Same as Jamaica.
➤Sweden: Sneaking
Same rules. It counts from one to five and turns around quickly.

►Poland: Hide and Seek

Same rules as Wales except the group chooses It by singing a rhyme like "Abra-cadabra, wizzy woo, I can fly and so can you," then everyone points to the chosen player.

►Peru: One-Two-Three O'clock

FIGURE 1.24   . . . he quickly turns . . .

One player is It and faces away from the other players, who start on a line about twenty-five feet away. When It calls out "One-Two-Three," all players can walk forward. As soon as It says "O'clock!" he quickly turns around to catch any player still moving. Any player who is caught moving, even slightly, must stand motionless on the spot where he was caught. The game continues with the remaining active players. As soon as one player makes it all the way to the line, touches It, and says "One-Two-Three O'clock," they change positions and the game starts over.

►►DROP THE HANKY

Country: China
Type: Running
Players: 16 or more
Age: 6–9
Equipment: Piece of cloth

In a very old book, *A Little Pretty Pocker-Book* (1774) a young player is described as dropping a letter, not a handkerchief, behind one of the young ladies in a circle while everyone sang:

> I sent a letter to my love
> And on the way I dropped it.
> I dropped it once, I dropped it twice,
> I dropped it three times over,
> Shut your eyes, look at the skies,
> Guess where the letter lies.

Other references to the game appear throughout the centuries, in England as well as in many other countries. Today, it is still popular on all six continents.

➤➤HOW TO PLAY

Arrange six to fifteen players, sitting in a circle and facing toward the center. Next, one player is chosen to be It and is given the piece of cloth as the hanky. It walks around the outside of the circle while the others sing and clap their hands. After a few moments, It drops the hanky behind a player and continues around the circle. If the seated player real-

FIGURE 1.25   . . . it drops the hanky . . .

izes the hanky has been dropped behind him, he picks up the cloth and chases It around the circle. If It gets to the player's place before the player, she takes his place in the circle and the player becomes It. However, if It is tagged before reaching the empty space, she is given the hanky again and continues to be It. Another situation results if the seated player does not realize the hanky has been dropped behind him. If this is the case, It runs around the circle then picks up the cloth still lying behind the seated player and hits him with it. These players then exchange positions and the game continues.

➤➤VARIATIONS

➤England
Same name, same rules.

➤Thailand: Mon Son Pha
Same rules.

➤Luxembourg
Same name, same rules.

➤Italy: Il Gioco Del Caterchio (Circle Game)
One child is placed in the center of the circle to clap her hands quickly or slowly. The It player must move around the outside of the circle in time to the rhythm of the clapping. When the center player stops clapping, the outside player must touch the shoulder of the nearest child seated in the circle. The game continues as above.

➤France: La Chandelle (The Candle)
The game is similar to the one played in China with a few changes in the rules. It is called the Mailman. The Mailman drops the hanky behind a player and says, "The Mailman has come." If the Mailman can run around the circle and back to the empty space without being tagged, the other player becomes the new Mailman and the game goes on as before. However, if the player with the cloth touches the Mailman before he reaches the empty space, the Mailman goes to the center of the circle. While he is standing in the center, the other children sing:

> Close the little peas
> The Mailman has not come
> He will come tomorrow morning
> One o'clock, two o'clock, . . . sing to twelve o'clock.

**FIGURE 1.26
La Chandelle**

After the rhyme, the old Mailman takes the player's position and the tagged player becomes the new Mailman.

➤➤STINGER

Country: South Africa
Type: Run and Tag
Players: 16 or more
Age: 8–12
Equipment: Utility ball
and a traffic cone

➤➤HOW TO PLAY

In a designated playing area, players form a circle with their legs apart. A traffic cone or similar object is placed in the center of the circle. One player throws the ball at the cone and tries to hit

FIGURE 1.27   . . . throws the ball at . . .

it; if he misses, he tries again. The ball then rolls off the traffic cone toward any player. The player who is touched by the ball is It and picks up the ball and starts counting aloud to ten. As soon as he starts counting, the other players run anywhere within the designated playing area. At the count of ten all players must stop moving. It throws the ball at any player attempting to hit him below the waist. Players may use their fists to prevent the ball from touching their bodies, but if the ball does touch any other part of their bodies, they become Its helpers. Once this happens, the player with the ball is no longer allowed to run with it. He may throw it at a free player or to another It player in order to get a better throwing position. The game ends when all players have been hit.

➤➤LEMON, LEMON

Country: Belgium
Type: Running
Players: 10–12
Age: 7–10
Equipment: Chairs

➤➤HOW TO PLAY

Players are arranged in pairs and each pair is given the name of any fruit, other than a lemon. The players sit on chairs in a circle with each pair sitting directly across from each other on opposite sides of the circle. One

FIGURE 1.28   . . . sitting directly across from . . .

player is chosen to be It and stands in the middle of the circle. When It shouts one, two, or three fruit names, these players have to exchange places with their partner. During the exchange, It tries to sit down on one of the chairs before the player gets to it. This leaves one person without a chair and he becomes the new It. When the middle player shouts "Lemon, Lemon!" *all* the players have to exchange places with their partners.

FIGURE 1.29   . . . having a base . . .

▶▶PRISONER'S BASE

Country: England
Type: Run and Tag
Players: 16 or more
Age: 8–12
Equipment: None

One of the earliest recordings of Prisoner's Base was during the reign of Edward III (1327–77). In those days it was known as "Base" or "Prisoner's Bar." Adults played the following version on the grounds of Westminster Palace with such exuberance that it interfered with parliamentary affairs and was banned by Edward III.

▶▶HOW TO PLAY

This game was described by J. Strutt in 1898:

> The performance of this pastime requires two parties of equal number, each of them having a base or home, as it is usually called, to themselves, at the distance of about twenty yards. The players then, on either side, take hold of hands and extend themselves in length, opposite to each other, as far as they conveniently can, always remembering that one of them must touch the base. When any one of them quits the hand of his fellow and runs into the field, which is called giving the chase, he is immediately followed by one of his opponents; he again is followed by a second from the former side, and he by a second opponent; and so on alternately, until as many are out as choose to run. Everyone pursues the man he first followed, and no other; and if he overtakes him near enough to touch him, his party claims one point toward their game and both return home. They run forth again and again in like manner, until the number is completed that decides the victory. This number is optional, and I am told rarely exceeds twenty. It is to be observed that every person on either side who touches another during the chase, claims one point for his party, and when many are out, it frequently happens that many are touched (Strutt, J., *Sports and Pastimes of the People of England*, London, Chatto and Windus, 1898, p. 144).

In Edward and Elizabeth Lucas' delightful book *Three Hundred Games and Pastimes,* written in 1903, the game became known as Chevy or Prisoner's Base, and with slight variations, it continues to be played in the same manner.

The game is started by one player (A1 = Bill) running out of his camp and calling "Chevy." As soon as Bill leaves Team A's camp, Jim (B1) calls out Bill's name and tries to tag him. The object of each Team A player is to get back to camp before his chaser from Team B can tag him, or to lure his chaser closer to Team A's camp. This is

FIGURE 1.30   "Chevy"

important because as soon as Jim, from Team B, starts to chase Bill, from Team A, another player from Team A, Mary (A2), can call out, run after, and tag Jim from Team B. A player from either team can only chase one player. If a player is caught, he goes to his opponent's prison. As soon as a player, for example Bill from Team A, is in Player B's prison, he calls out "Rescue!" When this happens, a player from Player A's camp calls "Prisoner!" and runs out to rescue him. As soon as this happens, a player from Team B's camp calls out the rescuer's name and tries to tag him before he reaches B's prison. If the rescuer is tagged, he becomes another prisoner. If he reaches the prison first, both members from Team A are given free passage back to their camp.

FIGURE 1.31   . . . and pretend to be . . .

▶▶EMERGENCY

Country: Canada
Type: Run and Tag
Players: 16 or more

Age: 8–12
Equipment: None

▶▶HOW TO PLAY

Two players are chosen to be It (Forces of Evil) and stand in the middle of the play-ing area. All other players are the Paramedics, and stand on the end line (Hospital Zone). It calls "Emergency!", which signals everyone to leave the Hospital Zone and run to the opposite end. The two It players try to tag as many Paramedics as possible before they reach the opposite end. If a player is tagged, she must lie down and pretend she is injured. In order for an injured player to be rescued, four play-ers must run and touch the injured player before being tagged. As soon as four un-tagged players have touched the injured player, they cannot be tagged until they have carried the injured player across the end line and reentered the playing area. After two or three minutes, the It players are changed and start the game over.

▶▶STEP ON MY SHADOW

Country: Botswana
Type: Run and Tag
Players: 16 or more
Age: 8–10
Equipment: None

FIGURE 1.32   . . . each player tries . . .

▶▶HOW TO PLAY

Mark off a playing area of about ten to fifteen meters square and have the group scatter within the area. On a signal from the leader, each player tries to step on as many other players' shadows as possible while keeping other players from step-ping on his own shadow.

▶▶ALLEY TAG

Country: Japan
Type: Run and Tag
Players: 16 or more
Age: 8–12
Equipment: None

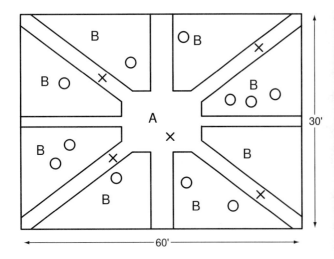

FIGURE 1.33   Alley Tag

FIGURE 1.34   . . . must leap over . . .

▶▶HOW TO PLAY

Arrange the playing area as shown in the diagram. Five players are chosen to be It and may move anywhere within area A. All remaining players must stay within the space designated as area B. On a signal from the teacher, the players in area B run clockwise around the playing area and try to get back to their starting positions without being tagged. Players must not touch alleys but may cross them with a leap. If a player is tagged or touches an alley, he joins the taggers in area A. As soon as the taggers have tagged ten players, five new It players are chosen by the leader and the game continues.

▶▶DIVISIBLE SNAKE

Country: Luxembourg
Type: Run and Tag
Players: 16 or more
Age: 7–10
Equipment: None

▶▶HOW TO PLAY

Two children are chosen to be the first Snake and hold hands while the remainder of the group scatters in the playing area. On a signal from

FIGURE 1.35   . . . and tag a fourth . . .

the leader, the Snake tries to tag other players. When a player is tagged, he must hold on to one of the taggers and they continue to try and tag a fourth player. Once a fourth player is tagged, the group divides into two and the game continues. The last two players to be caught become the new Snake and the game starts over.

▶▶MIC MAC RELAY

Country: France
Type: Run and Tag
Players: Class

FIGURE 1.36   Mic Mac Relay

Age: 9–12
Equipment: None

➤➤HOW TO PLAY

Arrange the class into groups of twelve players and number players as shown in the diagram. The game is played in the following four phases and the team that completes all four phases first wins the game. On a signal from the teacher the game starts with phase number one and continues to number four.

Phase One: Sideways Run: Ones run to twos, twos to threes, and so on until all players are back in their original positions.

Phase Two: Criss-Cross Exchange: Pair one and four exchange positions, followed by two and five, then three and six. (Note an error in the children's drawing.)

Phase Three: Little Bunches: Pair number ones run around the circle, pick up pair number twos, continue running around, pick up number threes, fours, fives, and sixes in the same fashion.

Phase Four: Caterpillar Race: As soon as pair sixes have been grabbed, they all squat down, hold each other's waists, and caterpillar walk to the finish line. If the line breaks, players must return to the original position and start again.

➤➤CARBONALES, CARDENALES, CARPINTEROS

Country: Peru
Type: Running
Players: 16 or more
Age: 8–12
Equipment: None

➤➤HOW TO PLAY

The leader is called Cardenale and stands on the end line. All other players are called Carbonales and stand behind the starting line. The space between the

FIGURE 1.37
"Carpinteros"

Carbonales and the Cardenale is known as Carpinteros. The leader calls out, "Cardenales!" and all players begin to run toward the end line. As they are running, the leader may call out, "Carpinteros!," which means all players must stop; or if Cardenale calls this out when they are already stopped they must remain motionless. If he calls out, "Carbonales!," players must move backwards. Any player who commits an error must return to the starting line. The first player to cross Carbonale's line takes his place and the game starts over.

▶▶KHO

Country: India
Type: Run and Tag
Players: 16 or more
Age: 8–12
Equipment: None

▶▶HOW TO PLAY

Arrange the class in a double circle, one behind the other and facing the center of the circle. One player is designated as the Chaser and another as the Runner. On the signal, "Go!" the Chaser tries to tag the Runner who runs in and out of the circle players. When the Runner stands in front of an inside circle player, she calls out "KHO," and the outside circle player becomes the new Runner. If a Runner is tagged before she can stand in front of a circle player, she must change positions with the Chaser.

▶▶ELECTRIC GATE

Country: China
Type: Run and Tag
Players: 16 or more
Age: 9–12
Equipment: None

FIGURE 1.38   . . . players from team A . . .

▶▶HOW TO PLAY

Divide the class into two equal teams and place each team on opposite lines. Two basketball standards are used as the Electric Gates. On a signal from the teacher, players from team A run out and try to touch team B's gate before getting tagged by a team B player. If any player on team A is tagged, he must remain in a "frozen" position. A player can be "unfrozen" by another player of his own team touching him, providing she "unfreezes" her teammate before she is tagged by the other team. The game continues until a player from team A touches the opponent's Electric Gate, or when all members of team A are frozen. The game starts over with members of team B running out to touch team A's Electric Gate.

▶▶FIVE AND TEN BALL

Country: Belgium
Type: Run and Tag
Players: 10–16
Age: 9–12
Equipment: 1 beanbag

▶▶HOW TO PLAY

All ten players sit in a circle. One player starts to pass the beanbag and calls himself Number One. The next child takes the beanbag and calls himself Number Two, and so on until the last number is called. When Number

FIGURE 1.39   . . . and throws the beanbag . . .

Ten calls out his number, he has to stand up and throw the beanbag to Number Five. Number Five stands up and begins to run around the circle to try and tag Number Ten. When Number Ten finally gets touched, they sit down at any place in the circle, and Number Ten starts counting again from One and passing the beanbag.

▶▶NUMBER RELAY

Country: Brazil
Type: Running
Players: 16 or more
Age: 9–12
Equipment: Small objects for each team

▶▶HOW TO PLAY

Divide the group into two or more teams. Draw two sets of parallel circles in front of each team and place one small

FIGURE 1.40   . . . and transfers it to . . .

object in each circle. On a signal, the first player from each team runs to the first circle, picks up the object, and transfers it to the opposite circle. This player returns to the second circle of the first line, picks up the next object, and continues the process to the last circle. As soon as the first player has transferred the object to the last circle, he steps behind this circle then the next player on his team begins to transfer the objects. The first team to complete all their transfers wins the game.

►►LOABAT AL-HALOOS BIT TIMBE

Country: Bahrain
Type: Ball and Tag
Players: 5–7
Age: 8–12
Equipment: Small, soft ball

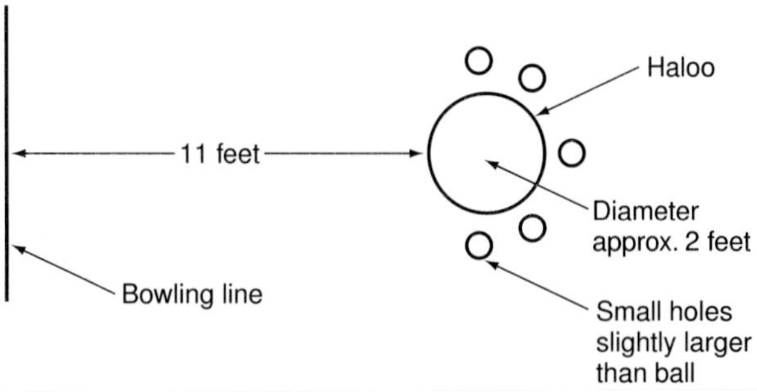

►►HOW TO PLAY

Substitute cardboard boxes for holes when playing indoors as shown in the diagram. The big hole (or large box) is called a *haloo.* One player stands behind the eleven-foot bowling line with the ball while the other players stand around the haloo. The player behind the line tries to bowl the ball into the haloo. If it goes in, the bowler runs and retrieves it while all other players run away from the haloo. As soon as the bowler retrieves the ball, he tries to hit any fleeing player. If successful, he rides on the back of the player who was hit. The player who was hit must carry the rider, pick up the ball, and try to bowl it into the large haloo. If the ball does not drop into any hole, the bowler must keep the rider on his back retrieve the ball, then try to bowl it into the large haloo. If the ball goes into the hole, the rider must get off, run and retrieve the ball, and try to hit any player as they run away. When the ball rolls into one of the smaller holes, the owner of that hole rides on the back of the bowler who, in turn, must retrieve the ball and try to bowl it into the larger hole. If the ball does not drop into any hole, the bowler must keep the rider on his back, retrieve the ball, then try to bowl the ball into the large haloo. If players run too far away from the haloo, set outer limits of the playing area.

FIGURE 1.41   Haloo is the big hole . . .

►►EYEGLASSES

Country: Korea
Type: Run and Tag
Players: 16 or more
Age: 7–10
Equipment: None

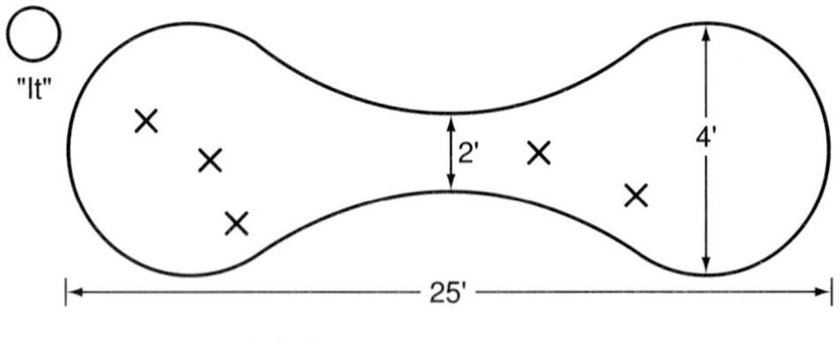

FIGURE 1.42   Eyeglasses

►►HOW TO PLAY

Draw a pattern in the shape of eyeglasses and allow all players to stand anywhere inside the Glasses. One child is chosen to be It and stands outside the Glasses. It tries to tag any player inside the Glasses or get her to step over a line. The Tagger may jump across the Glasses, but may not step inside. Players may move anywhere inside the boundaries of the Glasses. If a player is tagged or steps on the line of the Glasses, she becomes It. If one side of the Glasses becomes empty, It may jump into it and conquer it. When this occurs, a new It is chosen.

▶▶OPEN THE WINDOW

Country: Denmark
Type: Run and Tag
Players: 7
Age: 9–12
Equipment: None

FIGURE 1.43   . . . run up each side . . .

▶▶HOW TO PLAY

Three sets of partners line up behind a starting line. One player, the Window, stands ten feet in front of the first set of players and facing away from the line. When the Window calls "Open the Window," the two players at the end of the line run up each side of the line and in front of the Window. Once the players pass the Window, he tries to tag one of them before they can join together. If the Window tags a player, they exchange positions. The new set of partners returns to the front of the line. The game continues until everyone has had a turn.

▶▶CRAZY CIRCLE

Country: Spain
Type: Tag
Players: 8–10
Age: 9–12
Equipment: None

FIGURE 1.44   . . . so he touches it . . .

▶▶HOW TO PLAY

All players, except the one chosen to be It, join hands and form a circle. It stands in the middle of the circle and does not move from this position. On a signal, circle players must keep holding hands, then try to maneuver any player so he touches It. Once a player touches It, they change positions and the game continues.

▶▶CHICK CHICKABIDDY

Country: Estonia
Type: Run and Tag
Players: 6–8
Age: 6–9
Equipment: One small object

▶▶HOW TO PLAY

Arrange players sitting cross-legged in a circle and with both hands on their legs and palms facing up. One player is chosen to be the leader and stands in the middle of the circle, arms forward, palms down, and holding a small object hidden between his hands. He walks by each circle player and draws the palm of his hands over theirs, and says "Chick Chickabiddy do not show." When he returns to the center of the circle, he calls "Chick Chickabiddy come here." The circle player who received the small object raises it above his head and runs to the middle of the circle. As soon as he is recognized, all other circle players try to tag him before he reaches the center player. If tagged, the old leader repeats the game. If he reaches the center player without being tagged, he becomes the new leader.

➤➤CARRIAGE AND DRIVER

Country: Greece
Type: Run
Players: 16 or more
Age: 7–12
Equipment: None

FIGURE 1.45 . . . take short steps . . .

➤➤HOW TO PLAY

The group is arranged in partners who line up behind the starting line. A turning line is drawn twenty feet away. The player who is in the Carriage places his hands on the ground, arms extended, and legs spread apart. The Driver stands between the extended legs and grasps the partner's lower legs. On a signal, the Carriage takes short steps with his/her hands while the Driver follows with short walking steps. When partners reach the turning line, they exchange positions and return to the starting line. The first pair to reach the starting line wins the game.

➤➤LION IN THE DEN

FIGURE 1.46   Lion in the Den

Country: Nigeria
Type: Run and Tag
Players: 16 or more
Age: 6–10
Equipment: None

➤➤HOW TO PLAY

Draw a three-foot circle (Lion's Den) in the middle of the playing area. One player is chosen to be the Lion and sits in the middle of the Lion's Den. All other players run around the Den calling "Lion, lion come out of your den." At any moment, the Lion runs out and tries to tag as many players as he can. All tagged players become Lions and enter the Lion's Den. Each time the Lions leave the Den, the original Lion must leave first to start the chase. The last player to be caught becomes the new Lion.

➤➤WALL REFUGE

Country: Singapore
Type: Run and Tag
Players: 6–10
Age: 9–12
Equipment: None

➤➤HOW TO PLAY

This game is played near a building where there are several pillars or outdoor posts. Trees or fenceposts can also be used on the playing field. One player is It and all other players scatter around the playing area. When a player is tagged, she must hold on to a post. All other

FIGURE 1.47   . . . may rescue one . . .

players who are caught must also line up behind this player. Any player who is not caught may rescue one player at a time by touching the player who is touching the post. The last player to be caught wins the game and become the new It.

➤➤SUGAR AND HONEY

Country: Ghana
Type: Run
Players: 6 or more
Age: 6–9
Equipment: None

➤➤HOW TO PLAY

One player is chosen to be Sugar and another Honey. One half of the remaining players form a circle around Sugar and the other half around Honey. Each group begins to run around their leader and, at any moment, the leader signals the group to stop. The leader then asks the player closest to her who she prefers, Sugar or Honey. This player then moves behind the leader he/she chooses and places his/her hands around the leader's waist. The game continues until all players are holding on behind their chosen leader. If the number of players behind each team is uneven, take the player who was chosen first to be placed on the other team. Players on both teams must continue to hold on to the player's waist in front. Each leader then moves his/her team toward the other team. The opposing leaders join both hands and, on signal, each team attempts to pull the other team over. If a player releases his/her grip or if the team is pulled a distance of two feet, the other team is declared the winner.

➤➤OMLAR (NEED HELP)

Country: Iran
Type: Run and Tag
Players: 16 or more
Age: 9–12
Equipment: None

➤➤HOW TO PLAY

Divide the group into two equal teams. One team sits in a circle, elbows locked, and faces outward. Sitting players choose one of their teammates to be their

Guard, who then stands between his team and the circle players. The circle players must be about five meters away. On a signal from the Guard, the circle players try to reach the sitting players, grab their legs, and try to pull them so they have to release their grip and open the circle. Once the game

FIGURE 1.48   . . . and they try to pull them . . .

begins, the Guard tries to tag as many circle players as he can before one of his teammates loses his grip. Tagged players must return to their circle positions as soon as they are tagged. If all circle players are tagged by the Guard before any sitting player loses his grip, the sitting player wins the game. If any player loses his grip before all players are tagged, the circle players win the game.

▶▶CROSSCUT BEANCURD

Country: Hong Kong
Type: Running
Players: 5
Age: 7–9
Equipment: None

▶▶HOW TO PLAY

Draw a three-meter square and place one player on each corner and one in the middle. When the player in the middle calls "Crosscut the Beancurd," all players must leave and find a new corner. At the same time, the player in the middle also tries to find a corner. The player who cannot find a corner becomes the new middle player and starts the next game.

▶▶VARIATIONS

▶Going Shopping with Mother

The middle player signals all four players to follow her as she runs around the playing area imitating the activities of going shopping. When the Mother says "Go home now!", everyone runs to find a corner. The player who fails to find a corner becomes the new Mother.

▶Holding an Umbrella in the Rain

The four corner players hold up one hand as if they were holding an umbrella in the rain. On signal from the middle player, they all keep their hands in the air and begin to skip in place as if avoiding a puddle or being splashed by an oncoming vehicle. At any moment, the middle player can change the movement, such as hopping on one foot or jumping on both feet. Any player who stops performing the movement or performs the wrong skill becomes the new middle player.

▶▶SNAKE BRIDGES TO THE SEA

Country: Mexico
Type: Tag

FIGURE 1.49   . . . may decide, at any . . .

Players: 16 or more
Age: 9–12
Equipment: None

▶▶HOW TO PLAY

Two players form a bridge by joining raised hands. One is named Melon and the other Watermelon. One player is chosen to be the leader and all other players form a line behind him and hold on to the sides of the player in front. All players are secretly and randomly given the name Melon or Watermelon. The game begins with the two bridge players singing the following verse.

> To the sea Snake
> To the viper, viper of the sea, of the sea
> For here they can pass
> Those in the front run a lot
> The one in the back remains, back, back
> A Mexican girl is selling fruit
> Plums, apricots, melons, watermelons
> Verbena, verbena, garden of herbs
> Little bell of gold, let me pass
> With all my chickens, except the one at the back
> Back, back, it will be melon, it will be watermelon
> It will be the old woman of another day, day, day

As soon as the bridge players begin to sing, the leader starts to lead his line through the bridge. As the line passes under the bridge, the bridge players may decide, at any moment, to drop their arms around any player. They then ask the caught player, "Who do you go with—Melon or Watermelon?" If the caught player is a Melon, he moves behind the Melon bridge player. Now the line must pass through the first bridge then through the new bridge formed by the Melon and his first caught player. The game continues with the original bridge players randomly catching and asking, "Who do you go with?" As each player is caught and joins the new bridge, all remaining players in the line must pass through the original bridge and every new bridge. The game continues until all players have become new bridges.

▶▶CHASE IN ORDER

Country: Saudi Arabia
Type: Run and Tag
Players: 10–20
Age: 8–12
Equipment: None

▶▶HOW TO PLAY

The group is divided into two teams and each team is numbered from one on to the last player. Team A scatters in a thirty-foot playing area and Team B stands on one side of the square. The game begins with the leader calling out two numbers, such as two and four. As soon as the numbers are called, players two and four on Team B begin to chase and tag their opposite numbers. At the same moment, the leader starts to time how long it takes for the two players to be tagged. As soon as the players are tagged, they must move outside the playing area and the two players from Team B run back to their team and touch two new teammates. These players call out their numbers and start to run and tag their opposite numbers. The game continues until all members on Team A have been tagged. The team with the lowest time score wins the game. Once everyone understands the game, the leader can call out four or more numbers and keep progressing until he can call out "Everyone moves."

▶▶ONE, TWO, THREE

Country: Switzerland
Type: Run and Tag
Players: 16 or more
Age: 9–12
Equipment: None

FIGURE 1.50   . . . they try to tag . . .

➤➤HOW TO PLAY

One player is chosen to be It and stands in the middle of a large circle of players. Circle players are assigned a number by counting off one, two, three, around the circle. The game starts with It calling out a number, such as three. All players with this number must run counterclockwise around the circle and back to their own space in the circle. As the players are running around the circle, they try to tag the player in front. At the moment the player is tagged, the tagged player must call out "Tagged." The first player to be tagged becomes the new It and the game starts again.

There are two other variations played in Switzerland. The first is while players such as threes are running, another number such as one is called out. The second variation is when a player is tagged, he must return to his original position and keep running, jumping, or performing any other type of movement, until the last player is tagged.

➤➤ADD A MOVEMENT

Country: Syria
Type: Run and Tag
Players: 16 or more
Age: 7–10
Equipment: None

➤➤HOW TO PLAY

One player is chosen to be It and all other players scatter in the playing area. It begins to move in a certain way, such as skipping, as he tries to tag another player. When a player is tagged, she must immediately move behind It and move in the same way then add a new movement such as patting the top of her head. Each new tagged player adds a new movement until five players are tagged. A new It is chosen and the game is repeated, with the exception that any new movement must not copy any movement from the previous game.

 Chapter Two

SIMPLE BALL GAMES

Ball games have been played by children, youth, and adults since the beginning of recorded history. An Egyptian mural from a tomb located near Beni Hasan shows women throwing and catching a ball. Hieroglyphics and archeological artifacts provide evidence of various types of ball games played in early Roman, Greek, and Arabic civilizations. These games were played with roundish objects, such as stones, bones, and hides. Their games usually involved kicking, throwing, and rolling the ball toward a goal or target. In Central and South America, rubber was used to make solid and hollow balls nearly 600 years ago. Early indigenous people of North America made balls out of roots, seal hides, and stuffed animal bladders for a variety of tossing and kicking games. With the advent of inflated rubber and synthetic balls in the late nineteenth and early twentieth centuries, new games, particularly those involving bouncing and hitting the ball with the hand or an implement, began to show up in almost every part of the world.

The ball games provided in this chapter are normally classified as simple ball games requiring a ball, a few rules, and, at times, one or more pieces of small equipment. These games usually involve throwing and catching, bouncing or kicking the ball toward a target. Almost all of them involve a few simple rules, a time limit, and a winner and a loser.

►►SEVEN SINS

Country: Peru
Type: Ball
Players: 9–12
Age: 8–12
Equipment: utility ball

Name of Game	Country	Type	Players	Age	Equipment	Page
Seven Sins	Peru	Ball	9–12	8–12	Ball	36
Brunt	Germany	Ball	12–20	9–12	Ball, cones	38
Borden Ball	Canada	Ball	16 or more	9–12	Ball	38
Open Ball	New Zealand	Ball	16 or more	10–12	Ball, cones	39
Dodgeball	U.S.A.	Ball	16 or more	8–12	Ball	40
Crab Soccer	Italy	Ball	16 or more	8–12	Ball	42
Kitchen Ball	Botswana	Ball	16 or more	7–10	Ball	43
The Fly	France	Ball	5–6	8–12	Ball	43
Beat the Ball	England	Ball	6–12	7–12	Ball	44
Ulu Maika	U.S.A.	Ball	16 or more	7–12	Ball	44
Nirali Batel	India	Ball, Tag	16 or more	9–12	Ball	45
Kickball	Australia	Ball	3	9–12	Ball	45
Goal	Scotland	Ball	3	8–12	Ball, cone	46
Arquitos	Peru	Ball	3	8–12	Ball	46
Roll the Ball Home	Wales	Ball	3	9–12	Ball, goal	47
Hoop Tag	Australia	Ball	6	8–12	Ball, hoop	47
Twenty-Five	Zimbabwe	Ball	10–20	8–12	Ball	48
Oina in 6	Romania	Ball	6	7–12	Ball, stick	48
Shoot the Duck	Czech Repub	Ball	10–16	8–12	Balls, box	49
Countries of the World	Switzerland	Ball	6–15	7–12	Ball	50
Run Away Little Kitten	Mexico	Ball	2–6	7–12	Ball	50
Balls and Funnels	Greece	Ball	2–64	9–12	Ball, paper	51
Hitting the Snake	Nigeria	Ball	4	9–12	Ball, skittle	52
Circle Bounce	Israel	Ball	4	6–8	Ball, hoop	52
Squares	Poland	Ball	4	10–12	Ball	53
Countries	Syria	Ball	6–20	8–12	Ball	53
Beanbag Pass	Canada	Ball	2	6–8	Beanbags	54

FIGURE 2.1   . . . throws the ball into the air . . .

▶▶HOW TO PLAY

Player number one stands in the middle of a circle formed by the remaining players. All other players are numbered from two upward. Player Number One throws the ball into the air and simultaneously calls out the number of one of the circle players. As soon as a number, for example, two, is called, all other players run away from the circle. When Number Two catches the ball, he calls out "Stop!" and everyone must remain motionless. Player Number Two may now take three steps toward the nearest child and throw the ball at him. If that player is hit, he is charged with one Sin. The game starts over and continues in this fashion until a player has been hit seven times (Seven Sins). When this occurs, he is required to perform something, such as make a funny face or say a rhyme, and then change places with player Number One.

▶▶VARIATION

▶England: Three Bad Eggs

One player is chosen to be It and stands in the middle of the circle with a ball (tennis or utility ball). The rest of the players each pick the name of a color or make of car, and so forth. Then one member of the team calls out the selected colors to the person who is It. It throws the ball in the air and shouts out one of the colors, for example "Red," and the player with this color runs to get the ball. While she runs to get the ball the remaining team players run off to other parts of the playground, and keep running until It shouts "Stop!" Then the players must stop and stand still with their legs apart while the person with the ball tries to throw it between the legs of the nearest player. If the ball goes through his legs, that standing player gets One Bad Egg. When one of the players gets Three Bad Eggs, he becomes It.

FIGURE 2.2   . . . throws or kicks the ball . . .

▶▶BRUNT

Country: Germany
Type: Ball
Players: 12–20
Age: 8–12
Equipment: 1 ball, 4 traffic cones, and 1 hoop

▶▶HOW TO PLAY

Arrange two teams as shown in the drawing. The first player of team A throws or kicks the ball into the playing area and starts to run around the four markers. The markers can be traffic cones or gymnastic apparatus, such as vaulting horses, which the children like because of the next rule. The running player may stop at or on any marker and wait for the next throw by her teammate. Two or more players may wait at any marker. When a ball is thrown, players from team B try to catch it, then run and place it in the hoop and call out "Brunt!" If any player on team A is caught off any marker at the moment "Brunt" is called, and the teams change positions. One point is awarded for each completed trip around the four markers.

▶▶BORDEN BALL

Country: Canada
Type: Ball
Players: 16 or more
Age: 9–12
Equipment: 1 inflated ball

▶▶HOW TO PLAY

Place one goalie from each team in an eight-foot goal area in the center of each line (use two posts or traffic cones as goalposts). The object is to throw the ball

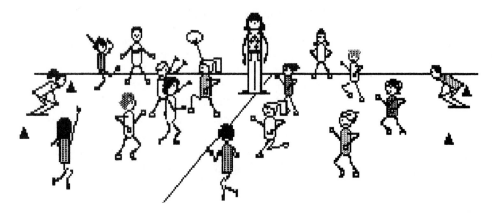

FIGURE 2.3   . . . may be thrown in any direction . . .

through the opponent's goal. The game begins with a jump ball between two opposing players at the center line. The ball may be thrown in any direction, but it may not be hit or kicked. A player may take a maximum of three steps and cannot hold the ball longer than three seconds. On penalties the ball is given to the nearest opponent. Members of the team that do not have possession of the ball may check the player with the ball, but they may not touch, hold, or push him. One point is awarded for each goal. After a point is scored, at halftime, or at any official stopping of play, restart play with a jump ball at the center. If the ball goes outside of the sidelines, a player on the opposing team throws it into the field of play.

➤➤OPEN BALL

Country: New Zealand
Type: Ball
Players: 16 or more
Age: 10–12
Equipment: 1 ball, 2 goals (traffic cones)

FIGURE 2.4   . . . players may also run with the ball . . .

▶▶HOW TO PLAY

The class is divided into two equal teams. The aim of the game is for each team to get the ball through their opponent's unguarded goal. The starting team, selected by a jump ball, may pass the ball by hitting it with their hands or kicking it with their feet. These players may also run with the ball until they are tagged by the opposing team. When this happens, they must immediately, and without looking, throw it backwards over their head. The team that catches the ball resumes the play toward their opponent's goal. If any player catches a kicked ball before it bounces, she gets a free throw or kick at the goal. One point is awarded for each goal and the team with the highest number of points wins the game.

▶▶DODGEBALL

Country: United States
Type: Ball
Players: 16 or more
Age: 8–12
Equipment: 1 utility ball

▶▶HOW TO PLAY

One team forms a large circle, and the other team stands in the center of it. On a signal, circle players try to hit inside players below the waist with the ball. To avoid being hit, the inside players may move anywhere within the circle. Outside players may enter the circle to retrieve the ball; however, they may not throw at an opponent while inside the circle. Any player hit below the waist joins the outside circle. The last person remaining in the circle is the winner. Add two more balls according to the playing ability of the class.

▶▶VARIATIONS

▶Barbados: Dog and Geese Dodgeball
In this variation, the team in the center holds on to the waist of the player in front to form a chain. The object is for the circle players to hit the last player in the chain. All center team members must keep contact with each other and protect the end player from being hit. When the end player is hit, teams change positions and the game continues.

▶Estonia: Rectangular Dodgeball
The teams face off in rectangular courts as shown in the illustration. A captain for each team stands behind the end line of the opposing team. Each team tries to hit the opposing team below the waist. When a player is hit, he moves behind the opposing team's end line, and if he gets the ball, he continues to try and hit any player on the opposite team. The game ends when all players of either team are removed from their courts.

▶Jamaica: Dandy Shandy
Divide the class into two equal teams and toss a coin to decide which team will be in the bordered area first (the Dodgers). The other team spreads around the bordered area to retrieve balls for the two players chosen to be Throwers. Two or more balls can be used. The Throwers stand opposite each other and try to hit players inside the area with the balls. Any player hit with a ball is required to stand outside the bordered area and join the Throwers team as a Retriever. After all players are hit, the other team goes inside the bordered area, and the game is repeated. If the last player from any team dodges ten consecutive balls, her team is allowed to return to the bordered area and dodge balls again.

FIGURE 2.5   . . . to hit the last player . . .

FIGURE 2.6   Rectangular Dodgeball

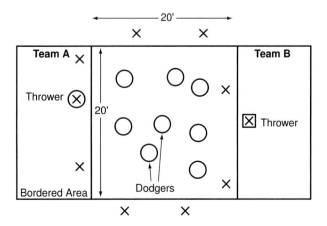

FIGURE 2.7   Dandy Shandy

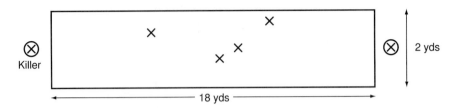

FIGURE 2.8   "Matagente"

►Peru: Matagente (Killers)

The players are arranged as shown in the diagram. The two outside players, The Killers, throw from behind the end line and try to hit other players below the waist. Killers may retrieve the ball from inside or outside the designated playing area but must return to their end line before throwing the ball. Inside players may move anywhere in the rectangular area. If a player is hit, the first time he loses his skin, the second time he loses one life, and the third time he is out of the game. If an inside player can catch a ball before it touches the ground, he gains one life. This player can keep this "spare" life or give it to another player who may have to leave the game.

FIGURE 2.9   . . . are always on all fours . . .

►►CALCIO SEDUTO (CRAB SOCCER)

Country: Italy
Type: Ball
Players: 16 or more
Age: 8–12
Equipment: 1 ball and 2 goals

►►HOW TO PLAY

Arrange the playing area as shown in the illustration. The rules are the same as regular soccer, with the goal posts (two yards between each post) but without the goal and out-of-bounds areas. The players are always on all fours in a crab walk position (balancing on the hands and feet with the back to the floor). Only the goalies can guard or touch the ball with their hands. The other players can only use their feet or heads to move the ball.

▶▶VARIATION

▶Peru: Futbol de Toros

This version is similar to the above game with a few enjoyable variations. Players begin in a crab walk position and may move the ball with hands, feet, or head. When the whistle blows, players turn over and must move on hands and feet. When the ball goes out of the circle, any opponent may retrieve it and bring it back to the place where it went out, and continue the game. Any time the whistle blows means a change in playing positions.

▶▶KITCHEN BALL

Country: Botswana
Type: Ball
Players: 16 or more
Age: 7–10
Equipment: 1 ball for each team

FIGURE 2.10   . . . in line with their feet apart . . .

▶▶HOW TO PLAY

Each team stands in a line with their feet apart. Player number one on each team holds the ball about chest high. On the signal, "Go," the ball is passed through their legs to the end player. The end player takes the ball to the front of the team and repeats the action. The team that finishes first wins the relay.

▶▶THE FLY

Country: France
Type: Ball
Players: 5–6
Age: 8–12
Equipment: 1 ball

FIGURE 2.11   . . . with their hands clasped together . . .

▶▶HOW TO PLAY

One player is designated as the Leader and holds the ball while all other players stand on a line with their hands clasped together. The Leader then throws the ball to one of the players who must try to catch it, throw it back, and immediately reclasp his or her hands. After two or three throws, the Leader begins to fake throws in order to tempt any player to release her hands in order to catch the ball. Every fair catch receives one Fly, and any player who opens her hands incorrectly is deducted one Fly. The player who gets to ten flies first changes positions with the Leader.

FIGURE 2.12   The bowler throws the . . .

➤➤BEAT THE BALL

Country: England
Type: Ball
Players: 6–12 on each team
Age: 7–12
Equipment: 1 small ball

➤➤HOW TO PLAY

Two teams are arranged as shown in the illustration. Four players on the fielding team form a stationary rectangle; the other players scatter in the playing area. The bowler throws the ball and the batter tries to hit it with his hand into the playing area, then run around the four stationary players. Any poorly thrown ball is rethrown. If the batter can run around all four players in the rectangle before the fielding team can field the ball and throw it to player one and sequentially around to player four, he scores one point. Each batter has a turn, then teams change positions.

➤➤ULU MAIKA (ROLLING STONE DISKS)

Country: United States (Hawaii)
Type: Ball
Players: 16 or more
Age: 7–12
Equipment: Softballs or similarly sized utility balls

➤➤HOW TO PLAY

"Ulu Maika" or "Olohu" was played in early Hawaii with rounded stones called *ulu*. Men used to either roll the stones as far as they could to show their strength or roll them through stakes to demonstrate their accuracy in bowling.

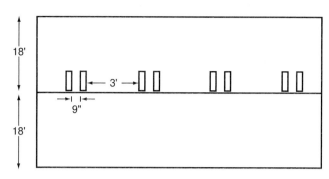

FIGURE 2.13   Ula Maika

Arrange players on opposite lines facing the two stakes. Each player tries to roll the ball through the two stakes. One point is scored for each time the ball rolls through the stakes without knocking them down. The game continues to a predetermined number such as eleven, fifteen, or twenty-one points. This game may be played with two players or as a team event involving two or more players on each team.

➤➤VARIATION

➤Ihe Pahee (Spear Sliding)

This is a similar game called "Ihe Pahee" or "Spear Sliding." The spears should be about five feet long (perhaps old broom handles) and rounded at each end. The game is played with the same rules as Ulu Maika except that each player tries to slide his spear through the stakes. Keep all players at least eighteen feet away from the stakes and not directly in line with the two stakes.

FIGURE 2.14   . . . slides the spear through . . .

➤➤NIRALI BATEL (KING)

Country: India
Type: Ball and tag
Players: 16 or more
Age: 9–12
Equipment: 1 ball

➤➤HOW TO PLAY

One player is chosen to start the game. He throws the ball and tries to hit another player. Players must remain inside the square (fifteen meters by fifteen meters) and use their fists to prevent their bodies from being hit. They also use their fists to hit the ball toward another player. Any player hit must move outside the square. If the ball goes out of the square, the last person to hit it, or any player who is out of the game, may retrieve it and throw it back into the square. Game continues until one player, the King, remains.

➤➤KICKBALL

Country: Australia
Type: Ball
Players: 3
Age: 9–12
Equipment: 1 ball

▶▶HOW TO PLAY

Three players stand behind a line about twenty feet away from a marker. On signal from the leader, they race to gain possession of the ball. The player who touches the ball first is the Shooter; the other two run to protect the marker. The Shooter may dribble around until she is ready to shoot. She is allowed one shot at the goal and, if she hits the marker, she scores one point and is given a bonus shot. This is a free kick taken three yards away from the marker and, while it is taken, the other two players must stand beside her. If she hits the marker, she receives another point and the game starts again. If she misses, the game begins again with all three starting with a race toward the ball.

FIGURE 2.15   . . . they race to gain possession . . .

▶▶GOAL

Country: Scotland
Type: Ball
Players: 3
Age: 8–12
Equipment: 1 soccer ball and 2 traffic cones

FIGURE 2.16   . . . shouts "Goal" just before . . .

▶▶HOW TO PLAY

The Goal is at one end of the playing area and Home is at the other end. One player is Goalkeeper and the other two players start from Home, dribbling and passing the ball. The player who is in the act of dribbling may not score; however, when he feels his partner is in a good position to score, he shouts, "Goal," just before he passes the ball to her. The player receiving the pass must shoot at the goal without any further dribbling. If the ball goes into the goal, each of the two field players gets one point. If the ball misses or if the Goalkeeper prevents it from going in, the Goalkeeper rushes out and tries to tag one of the players. If the player is tagged before he can reach Home, they exchange positions. If the Goalkeeper is unsuccessful, he goes back into the Goal and the game starts over.

▶▶ARQUITOS (LITTLE ARCHES)

Country: Peru
Type: Ball
Players: 3
Age: 8–12
Equipment: 1 soccer ball

▶▶HOW TO PLAY

Two players stand about six feet apart with their legs apart, facing the third player. The third player begins dribbling the ball toward the first player, and, when ready, attempts to kick the ball through the first player's legs. If successful, he scores one point and tries to score another goal against the second player. Players with their legs apart may use their hands to prevent the ball from going through their legs. If a player stops the ball, he changes positions with the third player and the game starts over. If a player scores the first two goals, he turns around with the ball and, while the other two players are facing away from him, tries to kick the ball so that it rolls through both players' legs. If successful, he gets two points for his double goal.

FIGURE 2.17   . . . and tries to score . . .

However, if the ball only goes through one player's legs, he does not receive a point and exchanges positions with the front player.

▶▶ROLL THE BALL HOME

Country: Wales
Type: Ball
Players: 3
Age: 9–12
Equipment: 1 soccer ball and 1 goal

▶▶HOW TO PLAY

Player A begins in goal and players B and C start about twenty feet away from the goal. Players B and C start dribbling and passing the ball and, as they approach

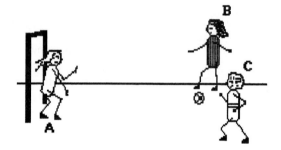

FIGURE 2.18   . . . start dribbling and passing . . .

player A, they try to dribble past her. They cannot kick the ball past player A. If a goal is scored, players B and C try again. If player A touches the ball before it is dribbled through the goal, she changes position with the player who was dribbling the ball at the moment the ball was touched.

▶▶HOOP TAG

Country: Australia
Type: Manipulative
Players: 6
Age: 8–12
Equipment: 1 tennis ball and 1 hoop

▶▶HOW TO PLAY

One player is chosen to be It and is given a hoop. The other players may move anywhere within the designated playing area and throw the ball back and forth to each other. If the ball is not caught in the air or after one bounce, the player who commits the error changes positions with It. If the player throwing the ball throws a poor pass, she changes positions with It. If It can place the hoop over a player who has possession of the ball, they exchange positions.

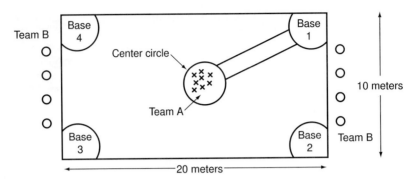

FIGURE 2.19   . . . Twenty-Five

▶▶TWENTY-FIVE

Country: Zimbabwe
Type: Ball
Players: 10–20
Age: 8–12
Equipment: 1 ball

▶▶HOW TO PLAY

Draw a playing court as shown in the accompanying diagram. Divide the players into two teams. Team A stands inside the center circle and Team B lines up on the opposite ends of the court. Play begins with a player on Team B throwing the ball across the court to one of his teammates. As soon as the ball is thrown, players on Team A run to any one of the four bases. At any moment, players on the bases may try to run clockwise to the next base. If they are hit with the ball while traveling toward the base, they are out and must move to the closest end line and join Team B. If they reach a base without being hit, they receive one point. Players are safe while remaining in base areas. Players on Team A continue to run clockwise and receive one point for each base they reach without being hit. The first player to gain 25 points frees all his teammates and the game continues until all players on Team A are eliminated. When this occurs, teams exchange positions and the game starts over.

▶▶OINA IN 6

Country: Romania
Type: Ball
Players: 6
Age: 7–12
Equipment: Stick and ball

"Oina in 6" is a traditional game in Romania, invented hundreds of years ago by shepherds. The official game is played with eleven players. However, the game described below is played by children 6–11 years of age, on smaller fields, and with simpler rules.

▶▶HOW TO PLAY

The referee throws the stick to the captain of one of the teams. This player catches it with one hand, then throws it to the captain of the other team who must catch the stick with one hand and above the place of the other captain's hand. This throwing is continued until one captain reaches the end of the stick first. His team becomes the batting team and the other team becomes the fielding team. The fielding team lines up on the side and end lines. One player of the fielding team throws the ball to the first batter. If the ball goes outside the side and end lines before being caught, the hitting team gets two points. If the ball is caught by the

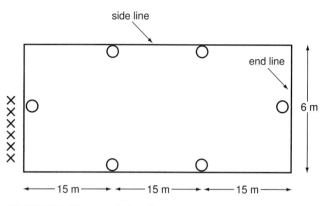

FIGURE 2.20   . . . "Oina"

fielding team, the hitting team only gets one point. After the first player hits the ball, he waits on the starting line until the ball is hit by player number two. At this moment, the first player runs toward the back line. If the ball is caught before it lands on the ground, the fielding team tries to hit the player who is running between the starting and end line. If any part of the runner is hit, the fielding team gets two points. The hitting team, however, may use their their hands to protect their head and face. As soon as a hitting player is hit, he must return to the starting line. Two players on the hitting team cannot be on the starting or end line at the same time. Teams change places when all of the batting team players are tagged out. The team with the highest number of points wins the game.

▶▶SHOOT THE DUCK

Country: Czech Republic
Type: Ball
Players: 10–16
Age: 8–12
Equipment: Large box, medicine ball, and small balls

FIGURE 2.21   The first team to knock the . . .

▶▶HOW TO PLAY

Place a large box on the center line and place a large ball (Duck) on top of the box. Two opposing teams stand behind their shooting lines. (The distance is determined by the age and ability of the children.) Each player has a small ball. On a signal, all players begin to throw their balls at the Duck and try to knock it off and over to the opposing side. As long as the Duck remains on top of the box, players may retrieve balls at any time but only from their own side. They must also return to their own starting line before throwing the ball. The first team to knock the Duck off the box is awarded one point. The game starts again and the first team to accumulate ten points wins the game.

▶▶COUNTRIES OF THE WORLD

Country: Switzerland
Type: Ball
Players: 6–15
Age: 7–12
Equipment: 1 small ball

▶▶HOW TO PLAY

One player is chosen to be the Thrower and is given a ball. All other players scatter in the playing area. Each player selects the name of a country (or animals, and so forth) but does not tell anyone what it is. When everyone is ready, the Thrower tosses the ball into the air and, at the same moment,

FIGURE 2.22   . . . must stand and form . . .

calls the name of a country. If any player has selected this name, he/she must run and fetch the ball. As soon as a player has possession of the ball, he/she calls "Stop," signaling all players to stop and face the new Thrower. The Thrower may then take three steps toward any player and asks him or her to select one of the following choices:

1. Stone: The player must stand and not move any part of his or her body.
2. Gum: The player must keep both feet on the floor, but can move any other part of his or her body.
3. Basket: The player must stand and form a basket with his or her arms.

If the player chooses Stone or Gum, the Thrower tries to hit the player with the ball. If he or she chooses Basket, the Thrower must try to throw the ball through the basket. If the Thrower is successful, the other player becomes the new Thrower and the game is repeated. If unsuccessful, the Thrower repeats the game, calling out a new country.

▶▶RUN AWAY LITTLE KITTEN

Country: Mexico
Type: Ball
Players: 2–6
Age: 7–12
Equipment: 1 small ball per player

▶▶HOW TO PLAY

The game consists of throwing and catching the ball as it is thrown against the wall. Each step described below becomes increasingly difficult. The first player begins with step one and continues throwing and catching and singing the verses through each step until she misses a step or the ball is dropped. As soon as a player misses a step or drops the ball, the next player in line takes his or her turn. When the last player has taken his or her turn, and providing no player has completed all the steps, the first player begins his or her next turn at the place where a step was missed or the ball was dropped. The first player to complete every step wins the game.

FIGURE 2.23 Throw and catch with . . .

Steps of the game:
    At a distance of one meter,

1. Throw and catch with two hands
2. Throw and catch with right hand
3. Throw and catch with left hand
4. Throw with right hand under right leg
5. Throw with left hand under left leg
6. Hop on left foot, right foot raised, and throw with two hands
7. Hop on right foot, left foot raised, and throw with two hands
8. Throw with right hand behind the back
9. Throw with left hand behind the back

Verse	Action			
Hit little kitten	Throw ball against wall and catch it with two hands			
Chocolate drink	"	"	"	"
Little table	"	"	"	"
A little more	"	"	"	"
One, two, three, for me	"	"	"	"
Halfway around	"	"	"	"
All the way around	"	"	"	"

Note: It is possible to increase the number of steps, the distance from the wall, and the difficulty of movements according to the ability of the children.

▶▶BALLS AND FUNNELS

Country: Greece
Type: Ball
Players: 2–4 per group
Age: 7–10
Equipment: 1 small ball per group and 4 pieces of paper

▶▶HOW TO PLAY

Four players stand two to three meters apart, holding a funnel made by rolling a piece of paper. One player holds a small ball (or a homemade paper ball) in the funnel. With the ball inside, he flicks it toward the next player, who, in turn, tries to catch the oncoming ball in his funnel. The game continues with the thrower always flicking the ball to a different player. As skill increases, repeat the game with everyone balancing on one foot, sitting cross-legged, or any other position the group can think up.

FIGURE 2.24 . . . he flicks the ball . . .

▶▶HITTING THE SNAKE

Country: Nigeria
Type: Ball
Players: 4
Age: 9–12
Equipment: 1 ball, 1 skittle, or small object

▶▶HOW TO PLAY

Draw a three-meter circle and place the skittle in the middle. One player is the Guard and may move anywhere inside the circle. The three other players must stay outside the circle and pass the ball back and forth until each player has caught it twice. The player who receives the last pass tries to hit the skittle while the Guard tries to protect it. Any player who hits the skittle becomes the new Guard and the old Guard joins the outside players. If the Guard accidentally knocks the skittle over, he changes places with the last player who threw the ball.

▶▶CIRCLE BOUNCE

Country: Israel
Type: Ball
Players: 4
Age: 6–8
Equipment: 1 hoop and 1 ball

▶▶HOW TO PLAY

Place the hoop on the floor and arrange four players around the hoop with one to two meters between each player. The game begins with the first player bouncing the ball to another player. When the ball gets back to the first player, she bounces it into the hoop and toward another player. The player who receives the ball continues the game by passing it on to another player. If a player makes a bad pass, drops the ball, or fails to

FIGURE 2.25 . . . the first player bounces the . . .

bounce the ball into the hoop, he is charged one point for the error. The player with the least number of points wins the game.

▶▶SQUARES

Country: Poland
Type: Ball
Players: 4
Age: 10–12
Equipment: 1 ball

▶▶HOW TO PLAY

Draw a playing area as shown in the diagram. Each square is named King, Rowie, Serwont, and Nedy. Moving in a clockwise order, players try to rotate to the King's square, the most important square. The

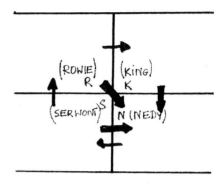

FIGURE 2.26   Squares

King starts the game by bouncing the ball in his own square then into any of the other three squares. The ball may bounce once or twice inside the receiving square. The player who receives the ball must use any part of his body except his hands to receive it. The receiving player is allowed to bounce the ball no more than three times before it is bounced to another square. If a player who is ranked higher than Nedy commits an error, such as hitting the ball with a foot, failing to bounce the ball the correct number of times, or failing to bounce the ball into a square, he must change positions. For example, if Serwont commits an error, he moves back to Nedy's position and everyone else moves clockwise to the next highest position. If Nedy commits an error, he remains in his own square and starts the game again. However, every time Nedy commits a fault he is charged with one point. When Nedy accumulates five points, he is out of the game and his square is taken over by the player in Serwont. The player in Serwont now defends both of these squares; however, he now can accumulate double the number of penalty points before he can be eliminated. He also may take double the number of bounces before bouncing the ball to one of the other two squares. If he accumulates ten points, he is out of the game, leaving King and Rowie to complete the game. If either King or Rowie accumulates five points, they are out of the game, leaving Serwont and the winner between King and Rowie to complete the game. The last two players use double the number of bounces and penalty points to complete the game. The last player remaining wins the game.

▶▶COUNTRIES

Country: Syria
Type: Ball
Players: 6–20
Age: 8–12
Equipment: 1 small ball

▶▶HOW TO PLAY

Mark off a three- to five-meter square playing area and draw a line across the middle of the playing area. Team A stands behind an end line. On the other side of the center line, players on Team B make holes slightly larger than the ball and give the holes a name of a country (or the name of a city). When everyone is ready, players on Team B stand behind their own hole. The first player on Team A tries to roll the ball into one of the holes. If the ball goes into one of the holes, players on Team A immediately start running anywhere within the playing area. The player behind the hole where the ball went in picks up the ball and tries to hit any player on Team A. If successful, players on Team B get one point. If unsuccessful, players on Team A get one point. The next player on Team B starts the second round of the game. If the ball does not go into the hole, the next player throws the ball, and so on until the last player has had a turn. Teams exchange positions after everyone has had a turn. The team with the highest score wins the game.

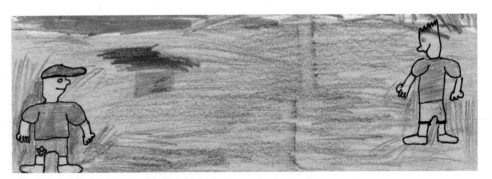

FIGURE 2.27   Beanbag Pass

➤➤BEANBAG PASS

Country: Canada
Type: Ball
Players: 2
Age: 6–8
Equipment: Beanbags

➤➤HOW TO PLAY

One player has a beanbag and tosses it under his legs to a partner. The partner repeats the same movement. On the second try the first partner attempts a new movement, such as throwing the beanbag over his head to his partner. The first partner has three tries at different movements, then the other partner takes his turn with three new movements.

Chapter Three

MANIPULATIVE AND GUESSING GAMES

One of the pictures on the ancient Egyptian tomb of Beni Hassan shows a player hiding his face while other players are holding clenched fists above his back. This is almost the same as the English game "Hot Cockles" and the French "Main-Chaude" ("Who Struck"). Another picture on the same tomb shows players flashing fingers that almost looks like "Rock, Scissors, Paper," a game currently played in all parts of the world. Historical records of other games like hopscotch, marbles, and gorodki date back to early Chinese, Russian, Egyptian, and Roman times. Over the centuries, these games involving guessing and manipulating small objects have been played by children and their parents with great skill and enjoyment.

Many of the games described in this chapter are similar to those played by children thousands of years ago. They may have different names and different rules, but they are essentially the same games. Other new arrivals, like "Gummi Twist," "Blind Snake," and "Yea String," are manipulative games that use modern inventions like elastic bands and plastic bottles.

➤➤GUMMI TWIST

Country: Germany
Type: Manipulative
Players: 3–4 per set
Age: 8–12
Equipment: Elastic band approximately nine feet long, with its ends tied. Use leg sections of panty hose as a substitute elastic band.

Name of Game	Country	Type	Players	Age	Equipment	Page
Gummi Twist	Germany	Manipulative	3–4	8–12	Elastic band	55
Telegram	Belgium	Guessing	6–15	7–12	None	57
We Are from Tihahana	Botswana	Manipulative	16 or more	8–10	Stones	58
Rocky Boat	Japan	Manipulative	7–8	10–12	None	58
Queenie I. O.	England	Mani + guess	5–7	6–9	Objects	59
Marbles	Greece	Manipulative	2–6	7–12	Marbles	60
Fivestone and Jacks	England	Manipulative	2–4	8–12	Jacks and ball	62
Klinkslagen	Belgium	Manipulative	2	10–12	Sticks	64
Giischt	Luxembourg	Manipulative	2–4	8–12	Sticks	65
Hopscotch	U.S.A.	Manipulative	2–4	7–12	Objects	65
Leapfrog	Scotland	Manipulative	16 or more	8–12	None	66
Rock, Scissors, Paper	England	Manipulative	16 or more	9–12	None	70
Rope-Skipping	Wales	Manipulative	2–20	6–12	Ropes	70
Easa Matessa	Scotland	Manipulative	5–10	7–10	None	72
Search for the Name	U.S.A.	Manipulative	16 or more	8–12	None	72
North, East, South, West	England	Manipulative	16 or more	8–10	None	73
The Jobs	Romania	Manipulative	16 or more	7–9	Small objects	73
La Tabla de Maní Picao	Cuba	Mani + guess	6 or more	7–10	Stones	74
Country and City	Israel	Manipulative	2–3	7–10	Cards	75
Blind Snake	Austria	Manipulative	3 or more	7–10	Blindfolds	76
Animals Have Horns	Nigeria	Guessing	5–9	7–10	None	76
Yea String	Singapore	Manipulative	4 or more	9–12	Strings	76
Bubble	Japan	Manipulative	8–10	6–8	None	77
Gypsy Wrestling	Spain	Manipulative	16 or more	9–12	None	77
Tampa	Brazil	Manipulative	4	10–12	Caps	77
Initiator	Poland	Guessing	6–8	7–10	None	78
Gorodki	Russia	Manipulative	2–4	10–12	Sticks	78

▶▶HOW TO PLAY

Two players stand inside the stretched elastic band. The band is around their ankles on the first round. The first player performs a series of jumping steps moving in and out of the banded area. Each player who follows must imitate all movements performed by the first player. If any player makes a mistake, he/she is replaced by the next player. When the first player takes his turn again (second round), the band is raised to knee high and the player may repeat his movements or create a new series of movements for each player to imitate. Variations from

FIGURE 3.1   Performs a series of jumping steps

other countries include: (1) changing the height to hip, armpits, and neck, (2) performing routines that include jumping on one foot and touching the hand with the other foot, and (3) performing routines with a partner or while holding a piece of equipment.

➤➤OTHER COUNTRIES PLAYING THIS GAME

➤Argentina: Elastic Band
Same rules.
➤Holland: Elastic Twist
Same rules.
➤Peru: Laliga
Same rules.
➤South Africa: Goommy
Same rules.

➤➤TELEGRAM

Country: Belgium
Type: Guessing
Players: 6–15
Age: 7–12
Equipment: None

FIGURE 3.2   "I'm sending a telegram to Mary"

➤➤HOW TO PLAY

One player is chosen to be It and stands in the middle of the circle as shown in the illustration. Circle players stand and hold hands. One player in the circle says, "I'm sending a telegram to Mary" (the name of a circle player), presses the hand on her right or left side, and calls out, "Started." The player who receives the pressed signal passes it on to the next circle player. This continues until it arrives at Mary, who says, "Arrived!" The center player tries to intercept the telegram by watching, and if he sees a person pressing the next player's hand, he says his/her name. If the center player is correct, he changes positions with the circle player.

▶▶WE ARE FROM TLHAHANA

Country: Botswana
Type: Manipulative
Players: 16 or more
Age: 8–10
Equipment: 1 small stone or object per player

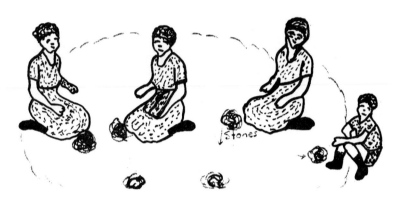

FIGURE 3.3   "We are from . . .

▶▶HOW TO PLAY

Children sit in a circle and hold a small stone in their right hand. They sing the song while holding on to their stone. When they sing the chorus, each player quickly places his stone on the ground in front of the player on his right. Each player tries to pick up the next stone as quickly as possible and place it in front of the person on his right side. Only one stone may be picked up at a time. The object is to try not to have any stones in front of you when the chorus of the following song ends.

> We are from tlha ba ne.
> [Re tswa kwa tlha ha ne]
>
> We are selling the goods.
> [Re ba pa tsa di lo]
>
> Repeat two lines.
>
> Chorus
> Do you want to sell the goods?
> [A o rata go re ki sa]
>
> Do you want to bury them?
> [A o rata go re-ka]

▶▶ROCKY BOAT

Country: Japan
Type: Manipulative
Players: 7–8 per team
Age: 10–12
Equipment: None

▶▶HOW TO PLAY

Arrange class into two equal teams. Player one of Team A leans against the wall and player two places his arms around player one's waist. All other players on Team A do the same. The first player on Team B jumps on the back of the last player and tries to move forward. Team A cannot attempt to force any player from Team B off their backs. However, if

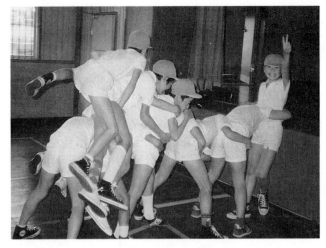

FIGURE 3.4   . . . player on team B jumps . . .

a player on Team B touches the floor after jumping on to Team A, he must return to his starting position and not move forward until the last player on his team has had his turn. Teams change positions and the team with the most players remaining on top wins the game.

▶▶QUEENIE I. O.

Country: England
Type: Manipulative and guessing
Players: 5–7
Age: 6–9
Equipment: Small object

▶▶HOW TO PLAY

Player A throws the ball or small object backward over her head in the direction of the other players. After throwing the object, player A remains facing away from them. When the object has

FIGURE 3.5   . . . throws the ball back over . . .

been caught and hidden away, usually in their hands behind their back, they begin to chant:

> Queenie I. O.
> Who's got the ball I. O.?
> It isn't in my pocket
> It isn't between my legs
> Hopscotch (They hop from one foot to the other)

When the chanting begins, player A turns around to guess who has the object. To further this aim, Player A may ask each player to turn around, which they must do, carefully hiding the object if they have it, or pretending to hide it if they haven't. Player A may also run through the group. If she does, the other players also turn around to conceal the small object as she passes through the group. After player A runs through the group, she must make a guess. If she guesses correctly, another turn is taken. If not, the person who has successfully concealed the ball takes player A's place.

►►MARBLES

Country: Greece
Type: Manipulative
Players: 2–6
Age: 7–12
Equipment: Marbles

Marbles has been one of the most popular and enduring games in the world. There is evidence that the game was played in ancient Egypt and pre-Christian Roman times. Each country has its own variation of the game and uses different terms to describe playing positions, rules, and the marbles themselves. English children say *taws* while Americans use terms such as *steelies, jumbos,* and *peewees* to describe the variety of different sized marbles they use in their game. The following games, sent from four continents, illustrate the fun and excitement children reap from the many variations of this activity.

►►HOW TO PLAY

A circle about one quarter meter in diameter is drawn on the ground, and each player puts two or three marbles inside the circle. A second outer circle about two meters in diameter is drawn around the circle. The playing order is determined by each player throwing his shooting marble toward a line or wall two to four meters away. The player whose marble is closest to the line shoots first; the player whose marble is next closest shoots after him, and so on. The first player takes his shot from anywhere outside the circle and attempts to knock the marbles out of the inner circle. If he knocks one or more marbles out of the inner circle, he wins them and takes another shot from where his marble came to rest. If he fails to knock a marble out of the inner circle, his turns ends and he must leave his shooting marble where it stopped. The next player takes his turn and may shoot at any marble within either circle. Whenever a player's shooting marble hits another player's shooting marble, the latter must give him one marble. After all players have had a turn, the first player shoots from where his marble last came to rest. The game ends when all marbles have been cleared from the inner circle. The winner is the player with the most marbles.

►►VARIATIONS

►Luxembourg: Smashers

The first player rolls his marble into a designated playing area (square or circle). Each succeeding player tries to hit any player's marble in the playing area. If successful, he keeps it and continues. If a player lost his marble in the previous round, he must start with his second marble from outside the playing area. Play continues until one player has won all the marbles.

►Japan: Five-Hole Marbles

The playing area has five small holes as shown in the diagram. Player number

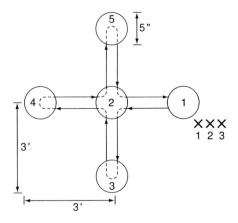

FIGURE 3.6   Five-Hole Marbles

one shoots from beside hole one and tries to roll his marble into hole two. If successful, the marble remains in the hole. The second player takes his turn and if he hits player number one's marble, providing it is not in the hole, player one is out of the game. Player two takes another turn. If player two's marble goes into the hole, player three takes his turn and the game continues until one of the players returns to hole number one.

FIGURE 3.7   tries to roll his marble as far as . . .

➤Peru: Road Runner

A pathway is drawn on any flat surface. Each player tries to roll his marble as far as he can without it going out-of-bounds. If it goes over the boundary lines, he is out of the game. The next player takes his turn and, if he hits another player's marble sitting in the pathway and knocks it out-of-bounds, that player is out of the game and the shooting player is given another turn. The first player to reach the finish line wins the game.

➤Ghana: Deng Deen

Draw a playing area as shown in the accompanying diagram. The first player tries to roll his marble into the square number one. If it lands inside the square, he picks it up, returns to the starting line, then tries to roll it into square number two. If successful, he continues the same pattern through square number six. If the marble does not land inside the square or on a line or rolls outside the square, the player loses his turn and must start with square number one on his next turn. The first player to successfully roll his marble into square number six wins the game.

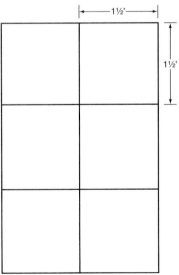

FIGURE 3.8   . . . the first player rolls his marble into . . .

➤Bahrain: Al-Koune

A small hole about one-half meter in diameter is dug three meters away from the starting line. Players decide on the number of rounds they wish to play. (In this game there are five rounds.) The first player shoots his marble toward the hole. If successful, it remains in the hole until the end of the fifth round when he takes another turn with his second marble. However, if the marble stops anywhere on the ground he loses his turn and the marble remains there until the end of the fifth round. Each player takes his turn until the end of the fifth round. The winner is the player who has the largest

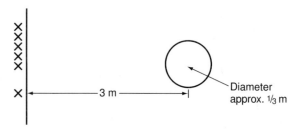

FIGURE 3.9 **. . . flicks his marble toward the hole . . .**

number of marbles in the hole, and wins all the remaining marbles left on the ground.

➤➤FIVESTONES AND JACKS

Country: England
Type: Manipulative
Players: 2–4
Age: 8–12
Equipment: 12 jacks and 1 rubber ball

Fivestones and Jacks are two very similar games that are derived from an ancient game called "Knucklebones." The "knucklebones" were fashioned from the bones of sheep. This game probably originated in Asia Minor long before it found its way into the ancient Greek and Roman empires. There is also evidence to indicate "Knucklebones" was introduced to other countries by Roman soldiers just as they did with hopscotch and marbles. Although Fivestones and Jacks have been designated as English games, they are also a favorite among young children in many parts of the world.

➤➤JACKS

➤➤HOW TO PLAY

This first version of Jacks is called "Onesies." The first player tosses the jacks on the ground. He then tosses the ball into the air, picks up one jack with the throwing hand, and catches the ball after it has bounced once. The jack is then transferred to the other hand. The ball is thrown up again and the process is repeated until all the jacks are picked up one at a time. When a player makes a mistake, such as failing to pick up a single jack, not letting the ball bounce, or failing to transfer the jack, he passes the ball and jacks to the next player. As skill increases, repeat the game, picking up two jacks at a time, then three, four, and so on until the player can pick up all the jacks at one time.

Other variations are (1) Eggs in the Basket: The nonthrowing hand is placed on the floor facing up and forming a cup between the fingers and thumb. Throw the ball up, pick up a jack, place it in the other cupped hand, and catch the ball after one bounce. Repeat the game in twos, threes, and so on. (2) Toad in the Hole: The nonthrowing hand is placed on the ground with the thumb and forefingers curled around to form a hole. Throw the ball into the air, pick up one jack, throw it through the hole, and catch the ball after one bounce. Repeat game in twos and threes, and so on. (3) Horses in the Stable: The nonthrowing hand is placed with fingertips and thumb arched and parted and touching the ground. Throw the ball into the air, pick up one jack, flick it into one Stable (between thumb and finger or

FIGURE 3.10   Eggs in the Basket

FIGURE 3.11   Toad in the Hole

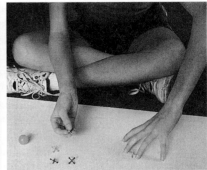

FIGURE 3.12   Horses in the Stable

finger and finger) and catch the ball after one bounce. After all jacks are in the Stables, reverse the process picking up one jack at a time from the Stables.

➤➤FIVESTONES (OR KNUCKLEBONES)

This game is played with five small rounded stones. The first player begins in a cross-legged or kneeling position and holds five stones in the palm of her hand. She tosses the five stones in the air, turns the tossing hand over, and tries to catch the stones on the back of her hand. She throws whatever number of stones are left and tries to catch them in the palm of her hand. The next player takes her turn and the player with the largest number of stones remaining in the palm of her hand starts "Onesies." If players end up in a tie, they repeat the basic throwing game until one player has a higher number of remaining stones.

Onesies The first player throws the stones on the ground, taking care that they land fairly close together and within arms' reach. She then picks up one stone, which is called the Jack, tosses it into the air, then picks

FIGURE 3.13   She tosses five stones in the air . . .

up one of the remaining stones and catches the Jack as it falls. The stone that was picked up is transferred to the free hand, then she throws the Jack up again and repeats the movement. This process is continued until all the stones are held in the free hand. If she fails to catch the Jack, drops a stone, or moves another stone as she is picking up one, she loses her turn. When she starts again, she must start from the beginning of "Onesies" on her next turn. The game continues with twos (pick up two at a time) threes (picks up three followed by one), and fours (pick up all four).

➤➤VARIATIONS

Fivestones can also be played in a way similar to Eggs in a Basket, Toad in the Hole, and Horses in the Stable.

➤Malawi: Kambabi

Players sit around a scooped-out hole that is about two feet in diameter. A handful of small stones are thrown into the hole by player number one. Next, she throws a large stone into the air and, before she catches it, must push all of the stones out of the hole. From here, she must throw the stone into the air again and push one stone back into the hole before she catches the stone. She continues returning them, one at a time, until the last stone has been pushed into the hole. After the last stone is pushed into the hole, she throws the stone up and pushes all the stones out again. The game continues with her returning the stones to the hole, two at a time, with each throw. This is followed by threes, and so on until all are returned with one push. If player number one makes a mistake during any part of this game, the next player is given her turn.

FIGURE 3.14   A handful of stones are thrown . . .

▶▶KLINKSLAGEN (CAT)

Country: Belgium
Type: Manipulative
Players: 2 per game
Age: 10–12
Equipment: 1 short stick and 1 long stick

▶▶HOW TO PLAY

The Cat (small stick) is placed against the brick (or a piece of wood) in such a way that the batsman can put the batting stick under the Cat in order to hurl it away (see diagram). Immediately after the Cat is lifted and hit (B + C), the batting stick is dropped on the

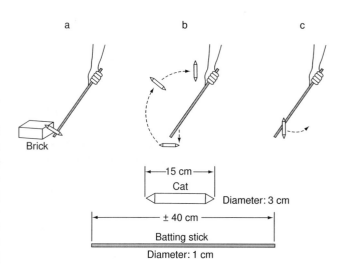

Diagram of Playing Area, Equipment, and Positions

FIGURE 3.15   Playing area, equipment, and positions

ground. The second player has to try to catch the Cat in the air. If the Cat is caught, then the batsman is out and the playing roles are reversed. If the catcher cannot catch the Cat, he has to throw it from the place where it landed and try to hit the batting stick where it was dropped by the batsman. If the batting stick is hit, the batsman is out and the playing roles are reversed.

If the second player doesn't hit the batting stick, the batsman gets three chances to hurl and hit the Cat as far as possible. The latter is done as follows: on the place where the Cat landed, the batsman tries to hit the Cat with the batting stick on the pointed end in such a way that the Cat rises in the air (see diagram B). While the Cat rises in the air, the player tries to hit it a second time to send it as far as possible (see diagram C). Measure the distance from the first hit to the landing position of the third hit. Now the playing roles are reversed and the second player repeats the above procedure. Measure the second player's distance. The longest distance wins the game.

FIGURE 3.16   Player B attempts to throw the giischt . . .

▶▶GIISCHT

Country: Luxembourg
Type: Manipulative
Players: 2–4
Age: 8–12
Equipment: 1 short stick (10 cm long) and 1 long stick (35 cm in length)

▶▶HOW TO PLAY

Player A with the long stick defends a one-meter square goal next to the wall. Player B holds the small stick (*giischt*) and stands behind a throwing line about three meters away. Player B attempts to throw his giischt into the small square. Player A tries to touch the giischt with his long stick before it lands in the goal; if the giischt falls somewhere outside of the goal area, he is awarded three hits at the giischt. A hit is performed by hitting the end of his long stick on the sharp end of the giischt to cause it to hop up. While the giischt is in the air, player A tries to hit it as far as possible. After two more hits, player A, using his long stick as a unit of measurement, measures the distance between the giischt and the goal area. Each player takes his turn and the winner is the one who has the highest score.

▶▶HOPSCOTCH

Country: United States
Type: Manipulative
Players: 2–4
Age: 7–12
Equipment: Small objects such as beads or buttons

Hopscotch is one of the oldest known games that children have played in nearly every part of the world. Although no one knows its origin, credit can be given to soldiers of the Roman empire for teaching the game to children

FIGURE 3.17   . . . one of the oldest games . . .

throughout Europe and Asia Minor. Throughout the centuries, each country added new versions, but, as illustrated, the game is still played in much the same way.

➤➤HOW TO PLAY

The first player stands on her right foot (this is her declared "hopping" foot and must be used throughout her turn), outside area one, holding the Puck (beanbag, button, etc.) in her hand. She tosses the Puck into area one, hops into this area, picks up the puck while balancing on her right leg, then hops out. She next throws the Puck into area two, hops back into area one, and then moves into areas two and three placing one foot in each area, straddling the two areas. In this position she picks up the Puck, hops into area two then one and out. This pattern is continued, hopping and landing with one foot in single spaces and with both feet in adjacent areas. Two hops are permitted in area ten in order to turn around. A player is out if she steps on a line, tosses the Puck onto a line or into the wrong area, changes feet on single hops, or touches her other foot on the ground during any hopping or retrieving movement. When a child commits an error, she goes to the back of the line.

➤➤VARIATIONS

➤French Hopscotch
The game follows the same basic rules of U.S. hopscotch with the player hopping on one foot in single squares and landing with both feet in adjacent squares. However, when a player lands with one foot in area seven and the other in area eight, he must jump up, turn around in the air, and land in the same areas.

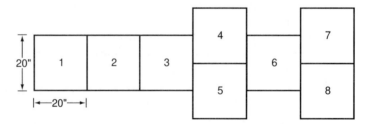

FIGURE 3.18   French Hopscotch

➤Italian Hopscotch
The first player stands on one foot outside square one, holding a Puck (beanbag, etc.) in his hand. He throws the Puck into square one and then hops into this area. Still standing on one foot, he kicks the Puck into square two, then hops into that square. He continues this pattern to square eight. When he reaches square eight,

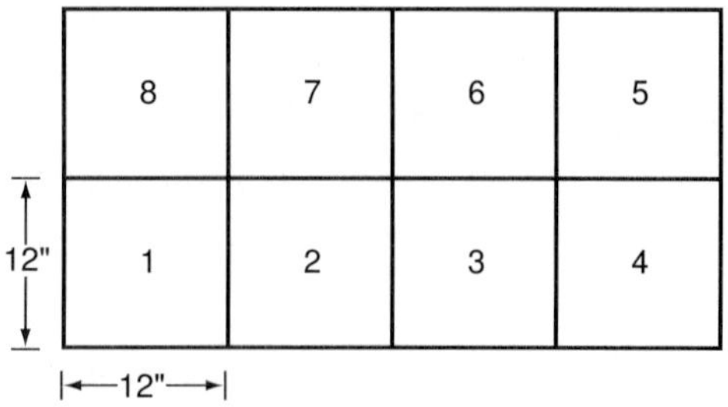

FIGURE 3.19   Italian Hopscotch

he places both feet on the ground, picks up the Puck, and hops backward through all squares to the starting position. A player is out if he steps on a line, if his Puck stops on a line, if he puts both feet down in any square except eight, or if he changes feet. When a child commits an error, he goes to the back of the line.

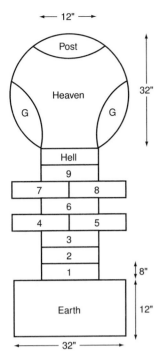

FIGURE 3.20 **Dutch Hopscotch**

►Dutch Hopscotch (Heaven and Earth Hopscotch)

Step 1: The first player stands on one foot inside the Earth square holding the Puck in her hand. She throws the Puck into square one, hops to square one, picks up the Puck, and hops back to Earth. She throws the Puck to square two, hops to square two, picks up the Puck and throws it back to Earth, then hops back to Earth. She continues the same pattern to square nine. Starting from Earth, she throws the Puck into Heaven; if it lands there, she hops to Heaven, picks up the Puck, throws it to nine, and follows the same procedure back to Earth. If the Puck lands in area Post, a player may not speak or laugh during her turn. If this rule is violated, a player loses her turn. If the Puck lands in area Hell, the player loses her turn and must start from the beginning when she takes her next turn. If the Puck lands in area six, a player may skip any one of the following steps:

Step 2: Instead of throwing the Puck, she can kick it from square to square with her foot.

Step 3: She can balance the Puck on her head as she hops through all the squares.

Step 4: She begins in the Earth square, but facing the opposite direction, and throws the Puck over her shoulder. If the Puck lands inside any square, it may be used throughout the game as a Safe House. The player can rest in this square on both feet and other players must skip this square during their turn. If a player makes a mistake during any part of the game, her turn ends and the next player begins. When a player starts her second turn, it begins where she made her last mistake.

►Peru: Kangaroo

The playing area is marked as shown in the diagram; each player takes a turn one after the other. The first player begins by facing the marked area and throwing a beanbag into area one. She then hops on one foot into each area and back to area one, picks up the beanbag, and hops out. This procedure is repeated for areas one to eight and back. If she does not throw the beanbag into the correct area, changes her hopping action, or fails to pick up the beanbag, she loses her turn. After all players have had their turn, each person starts again in the area where she made an error.

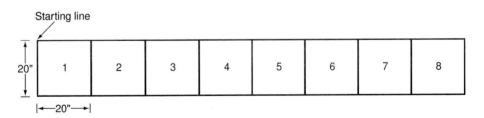

FIGURE 3.21 **Kangaroo layout**

The second phase of this game begins with the player throwing the beanbag into area one. Next, he hops into this area and, using the same foot he is standing on, pushes the beanbag into area two and so on to area eight and back to the starting position. If the beanbag goes out-of-bounds or if it does not stop inside each area, the player loses his turn. On his next turn, each player returns to the area where he made an error.

The third phase begins with the player holding the beanbag between her knees. Keeping the beanbag in this position, she jumps into each area one after the other and then back to the starting position. She cannot touch the beanbag with any other part of her body during this phase. If she drops the beanbag, lands on a line, or misses an area, she loses her turn. Like the previous two phases, on her next turn she returns to the area where she made an error.

►Zimbabwe: Tsetsetse

Draw a hopscotch pattern as shown on the accompanying drawing. Players print one word on each card, then place the cards on the rectangles or circle. The first player throws his stone into the first square on the left side, hops on one foot into the square, calls out the word printed on the card, then kicks the stone into the adjacent rectangle. This process is continued to the end rectangles and then back to the starting position.

FIGURE 3.22   . . . and kicks the stone . . .

A player loses her turn if she steps on a line, throws the stone on the line or outside the appropriate square or rectangle, or fails to read the correct word.

►►LEAPFROG

Country: Scotland
Type: Manipulative
Players: 16 or more
Age: 8–12
Equipment: None

FIGURE 3.23   . . . bend forward, place their hands . . .

▶▶HOW TO PLAY

Arrange the class into lines of six to eight players. All players except the last one bend forward, place their hands on their knees, and keep their heads down. The last player in each line runs forward, places his hands on the player's back, and straddle jumps over him. Once the last player in line has jumped over the player in front of him, the new "last player" stands up and begins his run and jumping action. The game continues until the first player in the line has finished jumping over all players and says, "Stop!" The children may decide to raise the height of the Frogs or change the distance between each player before starting the next game.

▶▶VARIATIONS

▶Belgium: Leapfrog

This game is played according to the same rules as above with one exception. When the last player reaches the front of the line, he may change the direction of the line. The line keeps on this new course until the next-to-the-last player reaches the front of the line, then he can change directions.

▶Italy: Circle Leapfrog

Children arrange themselves in pairs that are equal in terms of relative height and weight. Next, pairs form a double circle with the children on the inner circle assuming the leapfrog position facing toward the center of the circle. Outer players leap over their partners, crawl through their legs, repeat both actions again, then run clockwise around the circle. When they return to their places, they jump onto their partner's back and off, and exchange positions. The second partner repeats the actions of his partner. The first player to arrive back at his starting position and onto his partner's back wins the game.

▶Cuba: The Viola

One player is chosen to be the Donkey, who then bends forward, hands resting on his knees, legs slightly apart, and chin tucked forward and resting on his chest. All other players stand one behind the other behind a starting line located ten meters in front of the Donkey. A safety line is drawn ten meters on the other side of the Donkey. On a signal,

FIGURE 3.24   . . . place their hands on the Donkey's back . . .

they run forward, place their hands on the Donkey's back, and jump over without touching any other part of his body. As each player jumps over the donkey, he sings one line of the following rhyme.

> One my mule
> Two my watch
> Three my coffee
> Four my cat
> Five I punish you
> Six king's bread
> Seven the big knife
> Eight I cut your finger
> Nine I let you go

Ten is a small thing
Eleven bronze bell
Twelve an old woman
Thirteen a growing dwarf
Fourteen an old man coughing
Fifteen the lynx
Sixteen run away, the ox can catch you.

The players continue jumping over the Donkey and back to the starting line. At the moment a player sings "Sixteen run away, the ox can catch you," everyone runs to the safety line. As soon as they start to run, the Donkey tries to tag a player before he or she crosses the safety line. If a player is tagged, he or she changes positions and the game starts over. If no one is tagged, the original Donkey returns and the game starts over.

▶▶ROCK, SCISSORS, PAPER

Country: England
Type: Manipulative
Players: 16 or more
Age: 9–12
Equipment: None

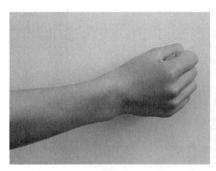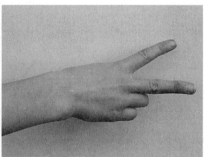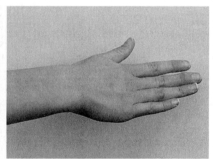

FIGURE 3.25   Rock, Scissors, Paper

▶▶HOW TO PLAY

Children first learn three symbolic gestures: (1) Rock = clenched fist, (2) Scissors = two fingers out simulating a pair of scissors, and (3) Paper = flat hand, palm facing down. Divide the playing area into two equal halves. Designate a center line and two end lines. Each team first decides which symbol to Throw (Rock, Scissors, or Paper), then lines up on opposite sides of the center line. Pecking order is: Rock breaks Scissors, Scissors cut Paper, and Paper covers Rock. When the teacher says "Go!", each team must Throw their symbols. The chosen symbols are thrown and the team that wins chases their opponents, attempting to tag them before they can cross their end line. A tagged player joins the team that tagged him.

▶▶ROPE-SKIPPING

Country: Wales
Type: Manipulative
Players: 2–20
Age: 6–12
Equipment: Small and large ropes

Rope-skipping, whether performed individually, with a partner, or large group, is enjoyed by children on every continent. It is, like hopscotch and marbles, a very old pastime with its own vocabulary of movement and age-old rhymes to accompany the various jumping movements.

FIGURE 3.26   Rope-Skipping

➤➤VARIATIONS

➤Barbados: "All in Together Girls"
Two players turn the rope and the first pair runs in and skips together. As they are skipping, all the other players sing:

> All in together girls
> This is fine weather girls
> When it comes to your birthday
> Please jump out.

At the end of the rhyme, they sing the months of the year. When the month each child was born is called, that player runs out. If either one of the jumpers makes a mistake they exchange positions with the rope turners.

➤China: Doubles
Two children begin standing side by side with the rope held in their outside hands. As they start jumping, one player turns out then back in followed by his partner repeating the movement. One player can also start skipping, then his partner enters and holds the waist of the jumper and both skip together.

FIGURE 3.27   . . . one turns out then . . .

►Canada: Group Jumping

Two children start turning a long rope. Other players enter one at a time until ten to twelve players are jumping together. A ball can be added to this game and passed overhead from the front jumper to the next jumper and on to the end of the line.

►►EASA MATESSA

Country: Scotland
Type: Manipulative
Players: 5–10
Age: 7–10
Equipment: None

►►HOW TO PLAY

To begin the game, all the players stand in a circle. One player is chosen to start. The other players stand with the palms of their hands facing the sky. The game progresses counterclockwise with the starter putting his right hand on

FIGURE 3.28   . . . player who says number five goes . . .

the next player's left palm. That person puts her right hand on the next person's left palm, and this continues around the circle. At the same time everyone says a rhyme that goes like this:

> Easa Matessa, oh, oh, oh.
> Crocodile Matessa oh, oh, oh, hello, hello.
> One, two, three, four, five.

The player who says number five goes into the middle. The game continues until there are only two players left. The person who does not go into the middle is the winner.

►►SEARCH FOR THE NAME

Country: United States
Type: Manipulative
Players: 16 or more
Age: 8–10
Equipment: None

►►HOW TO PLAY

Arrange the class into a circle formation, and place one player (It) in the middle. It keeps his eyes closed while the circle players move clockwise. When It feels ready, he calls "Stop," then walks forward to touch a circle player. It begins to feel the player's face and arms, and so on, and tries to guess the name of the person he is touching. If he guesses correctly, they exchange positions, and if wrong, he tries another player.

➤➤NORTH, SOUTH, EAST, WEST

Country: England
Type: Manipulative
Players: Class
Age: 8–10
Equipment: None

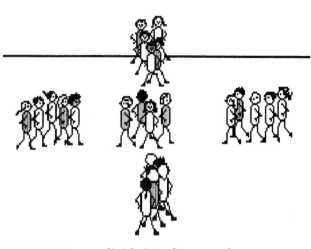

FIGURE 3.29   . . . divide into four equal groups . . .

➤➤HOW TO PLAY

Four children are chosen to be It and stand in the middle of the playing area. The remainder of the group divides into four equal teams and stands about four yards away from each compass point. The game begins with the leader saying, "North, South, East, West," and waiting about ten seconds to allow the four players in the middle to look around to see where every player in each team is located. After the ten seconds have elapsed, all four players must close their eyes for another ten seconds. During this time, all players within each team may change their position to another team. The teacher calls, "Open your eyes," and allows the North player to say where everyone on her compass point has come from. If she is correct, she remains in her position. The first player she fails to identify correctly changes positions with her. All other players in the middle complete their turn before the game starts again.

➤➤THE JOBS

Country: Romania
Type: Manipulative
Players: 16 or more
Age: 7–9
Equipment: 3 hoops, 1 brick, 1 piece of cloth, 1 plastic bottle

FIGURE 3.30   . . . the leader calls a word . . .

➤➤HOW TO PLAY

Divide the group into six equal teams and place on opposite end lines facing each other. Name each team on opposite end lines Builder, Doctors, and Tailors. Place a brick in the circles in front of the two opposing Builder teams, a plastic bottle in front of the two opposing Doctor teams, and a piece of cloth in front of the two opposing Tailor teams. When everyone is ready, the leader calls out a word, such as brick from one of the accompanying lists of words.

For "Builders"	For "Doctors"	For "Tailors"
brick	hospital	button
crane	aspirin	ironing machine
cement	receipt	cloth
shovel	thermometer	thread
sand	ambulance	needle
chalk	scalpel	thimble
mosaic	stethoscope	zipper

The first player from the two opposing builder teams runs to the circle. The first player to touch the circle wins one point. Both players return to the back of their line and the game continues. A player from any other team who runs out when his team name is not called loses one point. The team with the highest number of points wins the game.

►►LA TABLA DE MANÍ PICAO

Country: Cuba
Type: Manipulative and guessing
Players: 6 or more
Age: 7–10
Equipment: Small stone and marker

►►HOW TO PLAY

The group is divided into two teams that then line up on opposite lines drawn about four or five meters apart. Two boards are placed in front of the jumping line. Each team then chooses a leader. To start the game, the leader of team A is given

FIGURE 3.31   . . . tries to guess who is holding . . .

a stone. The leader and his teammates then move very close together and back to back in order to secretly pass the stone among themselves. When the leader calls out "To the plank of pitted peanuts," they all return to their line and extend their arms forward with their fists closed and say "Cao." When this happens, the leader of team B tries to guess who is holding the stone. If he identifies the correct player, his team gets the stone and a chance to jump over the board. The board is moved to where his heels land and the game is repeated with the leader of team B leading his team through the hiding phase. If the leader of any team chooses incorrectly, the opposing team gets the stone and a chance to jump over the board. Once a board is moved, the next player who follows starts his or her jump with toes behind the board. The first team to move the board to the designated finish line is the winner.

➤➤COUNTRY AND CITY

Country: Israel
Type: Manipulative
Players: 2–3
Age: 7–10
Equipment: Set of cards

➤➤HOW TO PLAY

Draw a playing area as shown in the accompanying diagram. When children are first learning this game, place the cards on the side of each square. Later, remove the cards and play with blank squares. The first player jumps into the first square and calls out "X." She jumps to the next square and calls out the name of a country. This process is continued to the last square. If the player makes it to the end square without making a mistake, she walks to the starting line and begins round two. However, if she fails to call out the correct word, or lands on a line, she is out, and must start from the beginning of the round on her next turn. In the second round, players repeat the jumping movements and call out each word twice. Each round adds one more repetition until round number five is reached. The first player to complete round number five wins the game. The game can be extended by starting round number six with a hopping movement and continuing to round number ten.

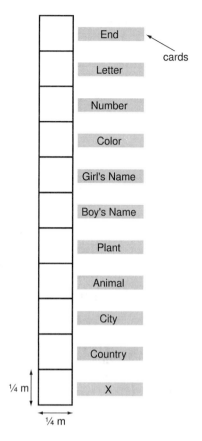

FIGURE 3.32   Country and City

➤➤BLIND SNAKE

Country: Austria
Type: Manipulative
Players: 3 or more
Age: 9–12
Equipment: Blindfolds

➤➤HOW TO PLAY

All the players stand in a row and everyone except the leader is blindfolded. Players place their hands on the shoulders of the player in front.

FIGURE 3.33   Blind Snake

The first player begins to walk forward and, when he approaches an obstacle, he makes a gesture, such as raising his left shoulder, to signal that he will be changing direction toward the left side. This movement is passed back from person to person. Other movements might be lowering oneself to a crouched position and signaling there is something to pass under or through. Players change positions and change type and positions of obstacles before leading the group.

➤➤ANIMALS HAVE HORNS

Country: Nigeria
Type: Guessing
Players: 5–9
Age: 7–10
Equipment: None

➤➤HOW TO PLAY

One player is named It and stands in front of the other players. All players then sit on the ground. It begins to call out the names of animals who have horns and players must immediately respond with the words "have horns." However, at any time It can call the name of an animal without horns. When this happens, players must remain silent. Any player who calls out "have horns" for an animal that does not have horns becomes the new It.

➤➤YEA STRING

Country: Singapore
Type: Manipulative
Players: 4 or more
Age: 9–12
Equipment: Long rubber string

➤➤HOW TO PLAY

Divide the players into teams A and B. Two players on team B hold the Yea string between them at floor level (Step 1). Player number one from team A jumps over the string and calls out "One." The string is then raised to knee level (Step 2), and player number one, without touching the string, attempts to jump over it. She repeats the same action with the string at waist level (Step 3). When the string is raised to armpit level (Step 4), player number one may grasp the string, pull it down, and jump over it. This is repeated at the shoulder (Step 5), ear (Step 6), head (Step 7), and one inch above the head (Step 8). If a player misses any one of the steps from one to eight, she is out of the game until a member of her team

FIGURE 3.34   Shelly

redeems her at Step 9. For Step 9 (called Shelly) the string is held at waist level and the player coils the string around her leg. If one or more players are out, and a player successfully reaches Step 9, all players return to the game and take their turns in order and after the last player on team A has had a turn. Each time all the players on team A complete Step 9, they receive one point. If all the players on team A fail to complete Step 9, they change positions with team B.

▶▶BUBBLE

Country: Japan
Type: Manipulative
Players: 8–10
Age: 6–8
Equipment: None

▶▶HOW TO PLAY

One player is selected to be It and sits on the floor with his knees bent. All the other players form a circle and hold hands. Circle players begin to sing a song and move in a clockwise direction. When the song is finished, all players must stop, sit down, bend their knees, and hide their faces on the top of their knees. Without moving his body or turning his head, It tries to guess who is directly behind him. If he guesses correctly, he exchanges positions with that player and the game starts again. If not, he remains in the middle and the game is repeated.

▶▶GYPSY WRESTLING

Country: Spain
Type: Manipulative
Players: 16 or more
Age: 9–12
Equipment: None

▶▶HOW TO PLAY

Players begin with right feet touching each other, left leg back and foot touching the floor. They grasp right hands, then try to push or pull until the other player's right or left foot is moved from its starting position. Repeat game with left feet touching and grasping left hands.

FIGURE 3.35 . . . with right feet touching each other . . .

▶▶TAMPA

Country: Brazil
Type: Manipulative
Players: 4
Age: 10–12
Equipment: Bottle caps

FIGURE 3.36 . . . with the middle finger placed against . . .

➤➤HOW TO PLAY

Tampa is a Portuguese word that means "bottle cap." Four players build a track on the ground and include a variety of obstacles such as slopes, bridges, and difficult curves. The first player places his Tampa behind the starting line and places his middle finger against the top side of his thumb. He then flicks the Tampa along the course. The next player takes his turn and, if he hits the opponent's cap, or if he goes outside the track, he loses his turn. The first player to cross the finish line wins the game.

➤➤INITIATOR

Country: Poland
Type: Guessing
Players: 6–8
Age: 7–10
Equipment: None

➤➤HOW TO PLAY

The players sit in a circle with their legs crossed. One player is chosen to be It and sits in the center of the circle. Circle players choose one player to be the Initiator. The Initiator starts the game by performing a movement that is immediately imitated by the other circle players. As soon as the first movement is performed, It is told to open her eyes and begin to guess who is the Initiator. When It makes the correct identification, they exchange places. A new Initiator is selected and the game continues.

➤➤GORODKI

Country: Russia
Type: Manipulative
Players: 2–4
Age: 10–12
Equipment: Throwing stick and pegs

➤➤HOW TO PLAY

If someone asked any person in any country what was Russia's national game, the answer would probably be chess. This is not true. Their national game is Gorodki, and dates back a thousand years to the early Slavic people. These people were farmers and did not have a taste for war, yet they had to defend themselves. To protect themselves, they lived in a *gorod* or fortress similar to the early stockade in the United States. During periods of peace, it was necessary for the men to remain physically fit as well as to practice throwing a spear—their chief weapon. They developed the game called "Gorodki," which consists of a circle marked on the ground or ice to represent the enemy's gorod. Inside the circle were placed wooden pegs representing Defenders. Players who knocked out the largest number of pegs with a wooden stick, which looked like a stone age club, with the least number of throws won the game. Throughout the centuries, the number of players, rules, and playing strategies have changed a hundred times over. Today, Gorodki is played by countless thousands of young and old people alike, in parks, school grounds, and backyards. The following brief description of "Gorodki" contains the basic skills and rules. The writer, however, has simplified the rules for younger children.

▶▶SKILLS AND RULES

The main skill in Gorodki is a sidearm throw of a weighted stick at five pegs located on a target square. The object of the game is try to knock all five pegs off the target in two throws. There are fifteen different sets or formations of five pegs, beginning with the simplest and progressing to the most difficult. The game may be played between two or four players.

▶▶PLAYING AREA

The playing area can be any flat surface (dirt, asphalt, or cement). The area immediately in front of the target square should be flat to allow the stick to hit the ground and slide toward the pegs, rather than bounce upward and away from the pegs. The area immediately behind the square should have some type of backboard (wire fence or high dirt wall) to catch the sticks or pegs. This is also an important safety feature that should be considered when introducing the game.

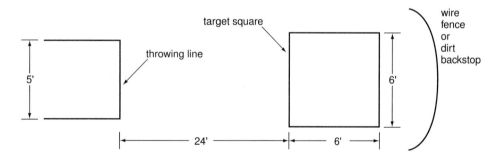

FIGURE 3.37   Playing Area

▶▶EQUIPMENT

Playing equipment (Figure 3.38) consists of two throwing sticks and five pegs. The throwing sticks can be any available small wooden or plastic sticks. The sticks should be banded with plastic or metal to give them strength or extra weight. The hand should be placed on the stick so that the center of gravity is toward the butt end.

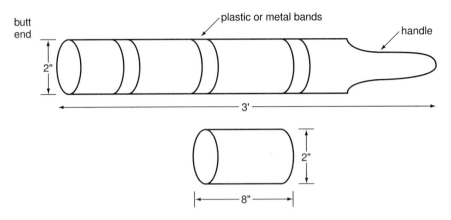

FIGURE 3.38   Equipment

➤➤SETS OR PEG FORMATIONS

There are fifteen different sets or peg formations, each with a special name. The layout of each set is provided in Figure 3.39. The dotted peg lines are provided as guidelines for arranging each formation.

Names of Sets

1. The Cannon
2. The Star
3. The Well
4. The Artillery
5. The Machine Gun

6. The Guards
7. The Shooting Range
8. The Fork
9. The Arrow
10. The Crankshaft

11. The Racket
12. The Lobster
13. The Sickle
14. The Airplane
15. The Envelope

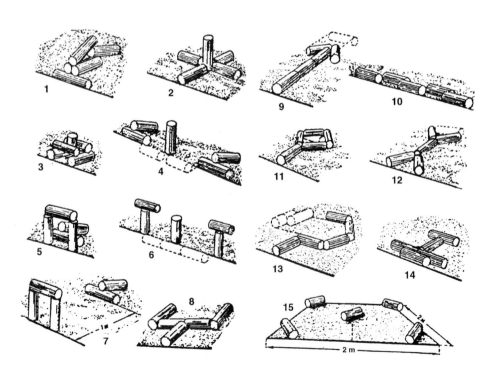

FIGURE 3.39   Sets or Peg Formations

▶▶THROWING SKILL

The basic throwing skill is a sidearm throw (Figure 3.40). The club should be gripped as if shaking hands and then drawn backward and upward behind the body. The forward motion should be a pulling action that draws the stick in a wide circular and forward motion. This movement should continue until the butt end of the stick is pointing in the direction of the pegs. It is then released. The club should rotate 360 degrees before it lands and strikes the pegs (Figure 3.41). A lot of practice is required in order that the club hit the pegs in a broadside fashion.

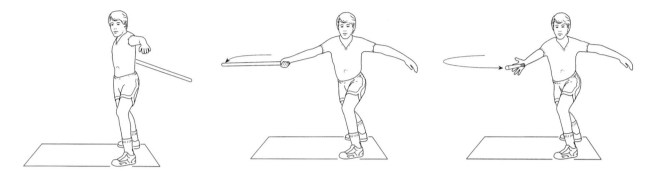

FIGURE 3.40   Throwing Skill

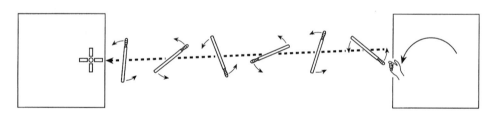

FIGURE 3.41   Movement of Sticks

▶▶SIMPLIFIED RULES

The following simplified rules and scoring system are provided as basic guidelines for introducing the game. The rules, distance, and equipment can be changed to accommodate local conditions.

Singles

1. A game consists of three to five sets of pegs.
2. Player A stands behind the throwing line and is given two throws at the first set of pegs. If he knocks all five pegs out on the first throw, he records five on his score sheet, then player B takes his turn. If one or more pegs are left after player A's first throw, he is allowed one more throw, then records his score. The pegs are reset and player B takes his turn.
3. The pegs must be hit completely out of the square to count.
4. Players continue rotation until all five peg formations are completed.
5. The winner is the player with the highest number of points.

Doubles

The game is played in the same way as singles with the exception that both players on team A have their turn before player one on team B takes his turn. To illustrate, if player one on team A leaves two pegs at the end of his second throw, player two on his team takes the second turn and tries to knock off the remaining two pegs. If player one on team A knocks all five pegs out on his first or second throw, player two does not have a turn. The pegs would be reset and player one on team B would take his turn.

Score Sheet

Score Sheet

	1 Cannon	2 Star	3 Well	4 Artillery	5 Machine Gun	Total
Player A	3	2	3	4	1	13
Player B	2	1	5	1	2	11

Part Two

NEW GAMES INVENTED BY CHILDREN

Chapter Four: New Games for Two to Five Players
Chapter Five: New Games for Six to Fifteen Players
Chapter Six: New Games for Sixteen or More Players
Chapter Seven: How to Help Children Create Their Own Games

During the past few years teachers have been using a problem-solving method to guide and encourage young children to create their own games. The key to this method is the manipulation of the four parts of a game, namely: (1) the number of players, (2) the available playing space, (3) type and amount of equipment, and (4) the skills and rules of the game in a problem-solving task children have to solve. For example, children are given a challenge, such as "Can you and your partner (two players) make up a game, in your own space (available playing area), using one ball (type and amount of equipment)? Your game must have a throw and a catch." (skills). They are then given a few minutes to design and play the game. Once the challenge is given to the group of children, there is no coaching or interference by the teacher. One set of partners might design a game in which they begin a few meters apart, then start moving in a circular fashion as they pass the ball back and forth. Another set of players may make up a game in which the first player bounces the ball to his partner and then pivots around on one foot while the other player catches the ball and repeats the same action. Each game that is produced is the result of the children's creative interpretation of the teacher's verbal challenge or task.

The games included in Part Two have all been created by children from the fifty participating countries. Each teacher was sent a series of challenges that were to be posed to her children. For example, the first challenge in Chapter 4 was presented to groups of children who were arranged in pairs. The challenge was "Make up a game that has two players, one ball, a throw and catch, and one goal." The games in Chapter Four, such as "Butterflies," "Bucket Ball," and "Magazine Ball," are examples of games children from different geographical and cultural backgrounds invented. The drawings made by some of the children indicate how well they understood the games they created, whereas the smiles and postures in the photographs show their enjoyment in playing their own games. Reactions from teachers were also very interesting. In most cases, they had never tried to get their students to invent their own games. In some situations, regardless of cultural or ethnic background, the children's first reaction to inventing their own games was quite negative. This is probably due to the fact that they were used to playing games that already had rules and boundaries, that is, those previously taught to them by older children or teachers. However, as they were gradually given the opportunity to exercise their creative abilities, they became very capable of inventing games that became more complex, challenging, and enjoyable to play.

➤➤➤Chapter Four

NEW GAMES FOR TWO TO FIVE PLAYERS

The games included in this chapter are the result of teachers from the participating countries posing the same challenges to their students. The initial challenges were kept as simple as possible to provide time for the teachers to get used to this method of teaching children. It also provided time for children to learn how to use their creative abilities in a very gradual and relaxed way.

The first challenge was, "Make up a game that has two players, a ball, a throw and a catch, and one goal." Starting with two rather than one player was done to allow for some initial sharing of ideas between players. In addition, providing only one ball, and specifying the type of skill and number of goals to be used, provided a reasonably easy structure to develop their first game. Children from different cultural backgrounds were equally creative in their approach to the first challenge. However, like their traditional games, there is an ever-present element of competition in each of their newly created games.

The next challenge was, "See if you can invent a game that has five players, passing a small object, and the game must have an element of surprise." This new challenge expanded the size of the group to five players. Because the task did not specify the type of pass to be used, each group had more freedom to determine whether they wanted to have a game that involved moving the ball with their hands or feet. The use of an unspecified object also allowed them to choose from a variety of locally available equipment, such as ball, stones, sticks, or beanbags. The last criterion in the challenge also specified that their new game had to include a rule or movement that produced the required element of surprise.

There are some games in the latter part of the chapter that involved four or five players. These games were created by a few teachers who designed their own challenges. This type of initiative is a positive sign that the participating teachers

Name of Game	Country	Type	Players	Age	Equipment	Page
Butterflies	England	Ball	2	7–8	Ball, box	87
Hit the Ball	Japan	Ball	2	9–12	Marbles, ball	87
Throw, Catch, Run	Scotland	Ball	2	8–12	Box, ball	87
Bucketball	Botswana	Ball	2	8–12	Ball, basket	88
Super-Duper Hoop	Australia	Ball	2	8–12	Ball, hoops	88
Hop, Skip, Jump	South Africa	Ball	2	8–12	Hoops, cones	88
Ball Catch	Wales	Ball	2	8–12	Ball, basket	89
Magazine Ball	Peru	Ball	2	8–12	Ball, magazine	89
Flying Goalie	France	Ball	2	10–12	Ball, goal	90
Catch a failing star	Canada	Ball	2	8–12	Ball, box	90
Skittleball	Belgium	Ball	2	10–12	Ball, cones	91
Trick the Guard	New Zealand	Ball	2	9–12	Ball, goal	92
Scoop Ball	U.S.A.	Ball	2	9–12	Ball, bottles	92
Ball in the Basket	England	Ball	2	6–8	Ball, basket	93
Two-Person Catch	Canada	Ball	2	7–10	Ball	93
Reaction Ball	Luxembourg	Ball	2	8–12	Ball, cones	94
Spacehopper Flight	Germany	Manipulative	2	8–10	Ball, darts	94
Quechibola	Peru	Ball	5	8–12	Balls	95
Catch a Caterpillar	England	Manipulative	5	9–12	Hoop, beanbag	95
Hidden Object	Botswana	Manipulative	5	8–10	Small object	96
Beanbag Tag	New Zealand	Tag	5	7–12	Beanbag	96
Twelve Big Eggs	Luxembourg	Manipulative	5	9–12	Ball	97
Quick Number	Japan	Ball	5	8–12	Beanbag	97
Surprise, Surprise	Wales	Ball	5	7–9	Ball	97
Back-Pass Beanbag	Australia	Manipulative	5	9–12	Beanbag	98
Paola Berni	Italy	Manipulative	5	9–12	Balloon, hoops	98
Through the Obstacle	Barbados	Manipulative	5	7–12	Ball, chair	99
One-Legged Concentration	South Africa	Ball	5	8–12	Ball, cones	100
Katter	Sweden	Manipulative	5	7–10	Small object	100
Spell and Catch	U.S.A.	Ball	5	8–12	Beanbag	101
Foot Searching	Belgium	Manipulative	5	9–12	Beanbag	101
Fir Cone Hide	Luxembourg	Manipulative	5	8–12	Cones	102
Pattywhack	Canada	Manipulative	5	8–12	Beanbag	102
Merry-Go-Round	Germany	Manipulative	5	8–12	Rope, beanbag	103
Bokstarsboll	Sweden	Manipulative	4–5	7–9	Ball, hoops	104
Double or Nothing	Zimbabwe	Ball	4	7–10	Ball, cans	104
Jogo Dotaco	Brazil	Ball	4	9–12	Bats, cans	104
Shoo Ball	Israel	Manipulative	2	6–7	Ball, cones	105
Pinball	Denmark	Ball	2	8–12	Ball, cones	105
Dangerous Circle	Romania	Ball	4	7–12	Hoops, ropes	106
Double the Fun	Czech Republic	Ball	4	7–12	Balls	106
Snatcher	Switzerland	Ball	5	9–12	Ball	106
Beanbag Polo	Mexico	Manipulative	4	9–12	Boxes, beanbags	108
Log Roller	Russia	Manipulative	2	9–12	Log	108
Shoot the Spinning Top	Israel	Ball	5	7–9	Balls, hoops	108
Name the Animal	Cuba	Ball	4	7–10	Ball, cards	109

saw value in this type of instruction and, according to several follow-up letters, planned to continue experimenting with this method with different age groups.

▶▶BUTTERFLIES

Country: England
Type: Ball
Players: 2

Age: 7–8
Equipment: Small ball and container

FIGURE 4.1   "A" throws to . . .

▶▶HOW TO PLAY

Two players sit on the floor, legs apart and feet touching. This position gave them the idea for the name "Butterflies." Player A throws to B and if B catches the ball, she has a chance to throw the ball into the container. If successful, she gets one point. If she fails to catch the ball, she retrieves it and throws it to player A, who then takes her turn. If the ball is thrown too high or too wide, it is returned to the thrower and rethrown.

▶▶HIT THE BALL

Country: Japan
Players: 2
Age: 9–12
Equipment: 2 markers and 2 utility balls

▶▶HOW TO PLAY

Player A stands behind the goal with a ball in his hands. Another ball is placed about two meters in front of the goal. Player B stands

FIGURE 4.2   . . . attempts to throw the ball . . .

about five meters in front of the goal. Player A throws the ball to B, who tries to catch it. If he fails to catch it, he must run after it and hold the ball where it finally stopped. Player B now attempts to throw his ball at the stationary ball located two meters in front of the goal and try to knock it into the goal. If player B fails to hit the stationary ball, or if it fails to roll into the goal, players change positions. One point is awarded for each successful goal.

▶▶THROW, CATCH, AND RUN

Country: Scotland
Type: Ball
Players: 2
Age: 8–10
Equipment: Small ball, box, and post

▶▶HOW TO PLAY

Arrange post, box, and throwing distance according to the children's level of skill. Player A

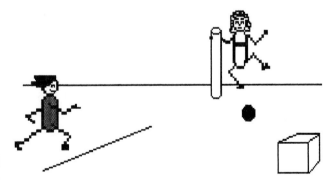

FIGURE 4.3   Player "B" throws the ball . . .

must hold on to the post and player B holds a ball and stands behind the throwing line. Player B throws the ball and if it lands and remains in the box, she gets one point and another try. Player A must remain at the post until the ball has landed in the box or on the ground. Player B throws the ball again and if it does not land and remain in the box, player B must fetch it and return it to the box before player A can run around the box and back to the post. If player A gets back first, they exchange positions. If player B gets back first, she gets another turn.

▶▶BUCKETBALL

Country: Botswana
Type: Ball
Players: 2
Age: 8–12
Equipment: 1 ball and 1 basket

▶▶HOW TO PLAY

FIGURE 4.4   . . . throws the ball from where . . .

Player A stands behind the basket with a ball. Player B stands behind the starting line. Player A throws the ball to B, who tries to catch it. Player B throws the ball, from where she caught or retrieved it, toward the basket. If the ball lands and remains in the basket, she scores one point and gets another turn. If she fails to score a goal, she changes positions with player A.

▶▶SUPER-DUPER HOOP

Country: Australia
Type: Ball and Tag
Players: 2
Age: 8–12
Equipment: 1 ball and 3 hoops

▶▶HOW TO PLAY

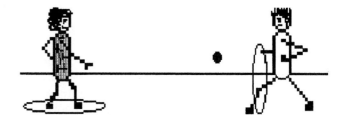

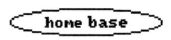

FIGURE 4.5   If the ball passes through a player . . .

Place two hoops on the ground about four to five meters apart. Player A stands in one hoop and throws the ball to player B, who holds the other hoop at her side. If the ball passes through player B's hoop, he drops the hoop and runs to home base and back. At the same time, player A runs after the ball, picks it up, and tries to hit player B below the waist before she can return to her hoop. If player B is successful, she is awarded one point and another turn. If unsuccessful, players exchange positions.

▶▶HOP, SKIP, JUMP

Country: South Africa
Type: Ball
Players: 2
Age: 8–12
Equipment: 4 hoops, 4 traffic cones, and a ball

➤➤HOW TO PLAY

Each player has a hoop on the ground and one balancing on top of two traffic cones. Player A stands in her own goal and throws a ball into player B's goal, then runs to her own hoop on the ground, and back to her original position. At the same time, player B runs from her hoop on the ground and attempts to retrieve the

FIGURE 4.6   . . . and throws the ball into . . .

ball and return to her hoop on the ground before player A gets back to her starting position. The first player back gets one point. Change positions after each throw. If a throw does not land in the hoop area, it is retaken by the same player.

➤➤BALL CATCH

Country: Wales
Type: Ball
Players: 2
Age: 8–10
Equipment: 1 small ball and 1 basket

FIGURE 4.7   If player "B" catches it . . .

➤➤HOW TO PLAY

Players stand about one meter on each side of a basket. Player A throws the ball to player B. If player B catches it, she receives one point. Then both players step backward one step. If a player misses the catch, she retrieves the ball, returns to her position, then steps back at the same time as her opponent. Players continue throwing, catching, and stepping backward until one player has five points. Players do not step backwards after a player has scored five points; however, the next time the player with five points catches a ball, he tries to throw it into the basket. One point is awarded for each ball that touches the basket and five points if it remains in the basket. The ball is returned to this player, who then throws it to the other player, and the game continues until one player has ten points.

➤➤MAGAZINE BALL

Country: Peru
Type: Ball
Players: 2
Age: 8–12
Equipment: Magazine, a ball, and a wastepaper basket

➤➤HOW TO PLAY

The first player stands behind a line about two meters away from the basket holding a ball on a magazine. He tries to throw the ball into the basket. If successful, he gets one point and another turn. If the ball fails to remain in the basket, players exchange positions. The first player to get five points wins the game.

▶▶FLYING GOALIE

Country: France
Type: Ball
Players: 2
Age: 10–12
Equipment: 1 goal and 1 ball

▶▶HOW TO PLAY

Two players start about twenty meters away from the goal (I). They begin to dribble and pass the ball back and forth until one player reaches the shooting line (about three meters from the goal) while he has possession of the ball (II). At this moment, he passes the ball to the

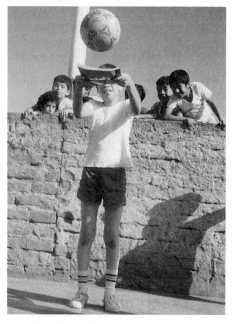

FIGURE 4.8   He tries to throw the ball . . .

other player and rushes to become the goalie (III). The player who receives the ball must try to score a goal before the other player gets into position, or after, by dribbling and attempting to score (IV). One point is earned for each successful goal; the first player to receive five points wins the game.

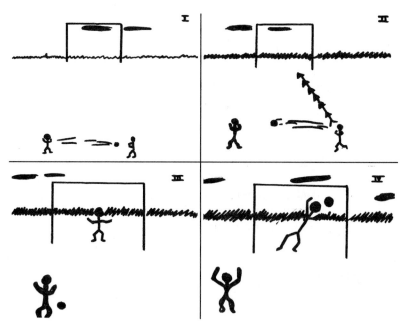

FIGURE 4.9   . . . they begin to dribble and . . .

▶▶CATCH A FALLING STAR

Country: Canada
Type: Ball
Players: 2
Age: 8–12
Equipment: 1 ball and small target (box or basket)

➤➤HOW TO PLAY

Draw or designate a rectangular playing area according to the playing ability of the children. Place a target on one end of the playing area. Player A stands beside the target and throws the ball upward so it will land in the designated playing area. If it goes out-of-bounds, it is re-taken. Player B starts from behind the opposite end of the playing area and tries to catch the ball before it lands in the playing area. If he catches the ball, he receives one point and a free throw at the target. If he hits the target, he gets another point and another turn. Player A must stand at least one meter away from the target while the free throw is taken. If he misses the catch or the target, the

FIGURE 4.10   Player "A" stands beside . . .

players change positions. The first player to score ten points wins the game.

➤➤SKITTLEBALL

Country: Belgium
Type: Ball
Players: 2
Age: 10–12
Equipment: 3 traffic cones and 1 ball

FIGURE 4.11   Skittleball

➤➤HOW TO PLAY

Arrange traffic cones as shown in the drawing. The object of this game is to try and hit the highest cone in such a way that the opponent cannot catch the ball before it hits the ground. If a player throws the ball and misses the target, the other player takes his turn. If a player throws the ball and hits the top traffic cone, and his opponent cannot catch it before it hits the ground, one point is awarded the thrower. However, if the opponent catches the ball, no point is awarded and players exchange positions. The player with the highest score at the end of the game is the winner.

▶▶TRICK THE GUARD

Country: New Zealand
Type: Ball
Players: 2
Age: 9–12
Equipment: 1 ball and 1 goal (any small container)

FIGURE 4.12   The Attacker dribbles the ball . . .

▶▶HOW TO PLAY

One player is the Attacker and the other is the Defender. The Attacker dribbles the ball with her hand within her own half of the playing area, until, with a dodge or feinting action to fool the defender, she throws the ball high into the opponent's half. She then runs and tries to catch the ball before it lands on the ground. The Defender cannot cross the line but can try to block the throw or intercept it before her opponent can retrieve it. If the Attacker catches the ball, she is given a free throw at the goal. Each player has five turns before exchanging positions. The winner is the player with the highest number of points at the end of the game.

▶▶SCOOP BALL

Country: United States
Type: Ball
Players: 2
Age: 9–12
Equipment: 1 ball, 2 plastic bleach bottles, and 2 hoops

FIGURE 4.13   . . . remain in their hoop . . .

▶▶HOW TO PLAY

Two players stand in their hoops which are about three to four meters apart. Each player has a Scoop made from an empty bleach bottle. Players must remain in their hoops and pass and catch the ball with their scoops. As one distance is mastered, change throwing hands or lengthen the distance between the hoops.

▶▶BALL IN THE BASKET

Country: England
Type: Ball
Players: 2
Age: 6–8
Equipment: 1 ball and 1 basket

FIGURE 4.14   If the ball lands and remains . . .

▶▶HOW TO PLAY

The player behind the basket throws the ball to her partner who is standing on the first throwing line. Mark throwing lines according to level of skill of the children. The partner who catches the ball attempts to throw it into the basket. If the ball lands and remains in the basket, she gets one point and moves back to the next throwing line. The throw is repeated and two points are awarded if it lands and remains in the basket. The game is repeated for lines three and four, and points are awarded according to each line. After the fourth line, positions are changed and the game continues. The player with the highest number of points wins the game.

▶▶TWO-PERSON CATCH

Country: Canada
Type: Ball
Players: 2
Age: 7–10
Equipment: 1 ball

▶▶HOW TO PLAY

The object of this game is to hit the target with the ball. The target may be marked on the wall or it may be any object that can be defended by the Goalie. The Shooter may take three attempts to score. Regardless of the outcome, the Goalie and the Shooter reverse roles after the Shooter's three tries. The game ends after a set time limit or after a set number of turns.

FIGURE 4.15   The "Shooter" may take three . . .

FIGURE 4.16   At the word "hop"

▶▶REACTION BALL

Country: Luxembourg
Type: Ball
Players: 2
Age: 8–12
Equipment: 1 ball and 2 traffic cones

▶▶HOW TO PLAY

Player A stands in the middle of his goal and faces away from the playing area. Player B starts about eight feet away with a ball and calls out "Hop!" before he throws the ball toward the goal. At the word "Hop!" the Goalie jumps around to face the shooter and in position to defend his goal. If Player B scores a goal, he gets one point and steps back to the next line and has another turn. If Player A catches the ball before it goes into the goal, Player B must move back to the next line and attempt his second shot at the goal from there without receiving a point. This process is continued for five lines; then players exchange positions. The player with the highest score wins the game.

▶▶SPACEHOPPER FLIGHT

Country: Germany
Type: Manipulative
Players: 2
Age: 8–10
Equipment: 2 space-hoppers and 2 darts or pieces of chalk

▶▶HOW TO PLAY

Each player sits on her spacehopper and holds a suction dart or piece of chalk. The object of this game is to attach the dart (or make a mark

FIGURE 4.17   . . . prevent the other player from . . .

with the chalk) on the opponent's spacehopper and to prevent the other player from attaching a dart to your spacehopper. One point is earned for each successful touch, and the first player to score five points wins the game.

▶▶QUECHIBOLA

Country: Peru
Type: Ball
Players: 5
Age: 8–12
Equipment: 2 balls

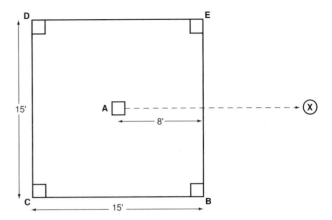

FIGURE 4.18   . . . player "A" . . .

▶▶HOW TO PLAY

Arrange the playing area as shown in the diagram. Adjust distances according to the level of playing ability. Player A has one ball in his hand and one on the ground. He counts "one, two, three," then kicks the ball away from the four marked areas. As soon as the ball is kicked, player E runs after it while player A runs with the other ball to player B. Player B takes the ball to player C while player A remains on player B's spot. Players C and D continue the pattern until player D reaches player A's spot and calls out, "Quechibola." If player E can fetch the ball and return to his spot and call "Quechibola" before player D reaches player A, he exchanges positions with player D. If player D reaches player A first, players A–D move one position counterclockwise and the game starts over.

▶▶CATCH A CATERPILLAR

Country: England
Type: Manipulative
Players: 5
Age: 9–12
Equipment: 4 hoops, 1 beanbag, and 1 stick

FIGURE 4.19   One player stands in the middle . . .

▶▶HOW TO PLAY

One player stands in the middle hoop and holds the stick in an upright position. The other four players stand inside their hoops. When ready, the outside players begin to pass the beanbag in a clockwise direction. When a player fails to catch the beanbag, the middle player holding the stick releases it. If the player who failed to catch the beanbag can grab the falling stick before it lands on the ground, he remains in his hoop. However, if he fails to catch the stick, he exchanges positions with the middle player.

➤➤HIDDEN OBJECT

Country: Botswana
Type: Manipulative
Players: 5
Age: 8–10
Equipment: Small object

FIGURE 4.20   Hidden Object

➤➤HOW TO PLAY

One player hides his eyes while four players hide a small object, then tell the lone player to open his eyes. The four players then begin singing any song they all know. While they are singing, the lone player begins to look for the object. If he moves closer to the hidden object, the others begin to sing louder; if he moves farther away, they sing softer. After the object is found, a new searcher is chosen and a new song must be selected by the group.

➤➤BEANBAG TAG

Country: New Zealand
Type: Tag
Players: 5
Age: 7–12
Equipment: 1 beanbag

➤➤HOW TO PLAY

Four players sit in a circle facing toward the center, eyes closed, and hands behind their backs. The fifth player walks around

FIGURE 4.21   . . . and place the beanbag . . .

the outside and places the beanbag in one of the player's hands. The fifth player keeps walking around the circle and, when ready, he calls, "Run to Safety!" All the players try to run to the designated safe area before the player with the beanbag can tag another player. If a player is tagged, he becomes the new fifth player.

➤➤TWELVE BIG EGGS

Country: Luxembourg
Type: Manipulative
Players: 5
Age: 9–12
Equipment: Medicine ball

➤➤HOW TO PLAY

Four players help the fifth onto a medicine ball. Once the player is standing on the ball, all the other players run around her and try to get her to fall off the ball. They cannot push her, but they can tickle her or make funny faces. When the player falls off the ball, she must say, "Humpty Dumpty Stop!" and allow the other players time to run away. On "Stop," each player must turn around and stand with legs apart. Humpty Dumpty tries to roll the ball through any player's legs. If successful, she receives one point. Player number two takes her turn, and so on, until one player has accumulated twelve points (twelve eggs).

➤➤QUICK NUMBER

Country: Japan
Type: Ball
Players: 5
Age: 8–12
Equipment: 1 beanbag

➤➤HOW TO PLAY

Players are numbered one to five and stand on a line five feet away from the wall. Player number one throws a beanbag against the wall and calls out a number. The player whose number is called rushes for the beanbag and calls, "Stop!" All the players stop and the player tries to hit one of the other players below the waist with the beanbag. The player that is hit becomes It and all other players return to the starting line for the next turn.

➤➤SURPRISE, SURPRISE

Country: Wales
Type: Ball
Players: 5
Age: 7–9
Equipment: 1 ball

➤➤HOW TO PLAY

Four players form a circle. The fifth player is designated to be It and stands in the middle. Circle players may throw or bounce the ball to any other circle player. If the middle player touches or catches the ball as it is being passed, he exchanges positions with the player who passed the ball.

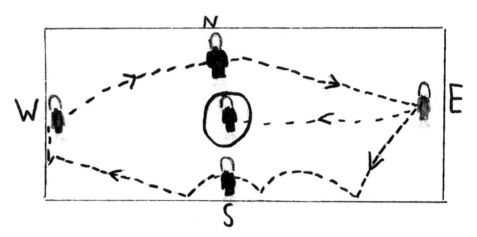

FIGURE 4.22   Surprise, surprise

➤➤BACK-PASS THE BEANBAG

Country: Australia
Type: Manipulative
Players: 5
Age: 9–12
Equipment: 1 beanbag

➤➤HOW TO PLAY

One person is It and stands about three meters away from the other four players. She faces the opposite direction and counts to twenty. The other players

FIGURE 4.23   . . . passing the beanbag . . .

stand with their hands behind their backs passing the beanbag from one to the other until It calls out "Twenty." On that cue, It tries to tag one of the players as they all run away, keeping their hands behind their backs, concealing the truth about which one of them has the beanbag. It must try to catch the player who has possession of the beanbag. During the game players may secretly pass the beanbag to each other. Once the player with the beanbag is caught, she becomes It. If a player is tagged and doesn't have the beanbag, then she can rejoin the game.

➤➤PAOLA BERNI (LOST ISLAND)

Country: Italy
Type: Manipulative
Players: 5
Age: 7–9
Equipment: 1 balloon and 5 hoops

➤➤HOW TO PLAY

Arrange the class into groups of five and locate each group in a designated area of the gymnasium. Each player lies beside his hoop (Island) and one of these players has a balloon. On a signal from the teacher, players begin to move on their stom-

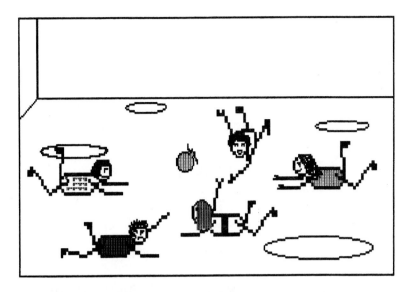

FIGURE 4.24   . . . move on their stomachs . . .

achs and keep hitting the balloon into the air. When the teacher calls "Home," players stand up and run to their hoop (Island). On the next turn, as the players are moving on their stomachs and hitting the balloon, the teacher removes one Island from each group. This time when she calls "Home," players run to any Island. The player who cannot find an Island is out of the game. The game continues until one player remains and is declared the winner.

►►THROUGH THE OBSTACLE

Country: Barbados
Type: Manipulative
Players: 5
Age: 7–12
Equipment: 1 ball, 1 chair, and a small object

FIGURE 4.25   Each player tries . . .

➤➤HOW TO PLAY

Five players line up behind a starting line. The distance is adjusted according to the level of ability of the children. At an appropriate distance away, a chair is placed facing the players with a small object (the target) sitting on the floor on the other side of the chair. Each player tries to roll the ball through the legs of the chair and hit the target. If a player hits the target, he gets one point and goes to the end of the line. The first player to receive five points wins the game.

➤➤ONE-LEGGED CONCENTRATION

Country: South Africa
Type: Ball
Players: 5
Age: 8–12
Equipment: 1 ball or beanbag and 4 traffic cones

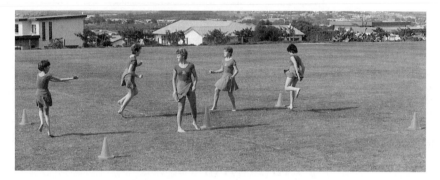

FIGURE 4.26   The player with the beanbag . . .

➤➤HOW TO PLAY

Arrange four traffic cones in a square; place one player in the middle of the square and each of the other four players next to a traffic cone. The player in the center has a beanbag and calls out, "Go!" Every player, including the center player, starts hopping on one leg to a different traffic cone. The player with the beanbag can throw it to another player at any time. Players cannot stop hopping until they reach another traffic cone, so they have to catch the beanbag while moving. If a fair throw is made and a player catches it, she gets one point. If she drops or misses the beanbag, she loses one point and must pick it up and throw it to another player. Two or more players cannot be at a cone at the same time. The game is restarted when all players are at a cone. The player who receives ten points first wins the game.

➤➤KATTER (CATS)

Country: Sweden
Type: Manipulative
Players: 5
Age: 7–10
Equipment: 1 small object

➤➤HOW TO PLAY

Four children sit cross-legged in a small circle. One player sits the same way in the center of the circle. The center player closes his eyes and counts out loud to ten while the circle players pass the beanbag behind their backs. The center player opens his eyes, remains in his sitting position, and tries to locate the child who has the beanbag. The circle players continue passing the beanbag, but if a play-er is caught with it, he exchanges places with the center player, and the game starts from the beginning.

FIGURE 4.27   The center player closes . . .

➤➤SPELL AND CATCH

Country: United States
Type: Ball
Players: 5
Age: 8–12
Equipment: 1 beanbag or ball

➤➤HOW TO PLAY

Five players form a circle with one player holding the ball. Before the game begins, each player must think of a word to be spelled. The game begins when player number one says his word, such as *elephant,* and calls out the first letter as he throws the ball to any circle player. The catching player must call out the second letter of the word before tossing the ball to another player. If he says the wrong letter, he tosses the ball and must run twice around the circle before rejoining the game. The next player must say the correct second letter, and so on, before the third letter is called out. Any word chosen must be more than five letters. This provides for the final rule that all players must participate in at least one letter of each word. Repeat game for each player's word.

➤➤FOOT SEARCHING

Country: Belgium
Type: Manipulative
Players: 5
Age: 9–12
Equipment: 1 beanbag

FIGURE 4.28   Foot Searching

➤➤**HOW TO PLAY**

Five players lie on their backs, one behind the other, in a straight line. The children pass a beanbag backward with their feet. If a player drops the beanbag, it is returned to the front player and the game continues. When the beanbag arrives at the last child, this player runs to the beginning of the row, lies down, and the game starts again. The game is over when the first child arrives again at the beginning of the row.

➤➤FIR CONE HIDE

Country: Luxembourg
Type: Manipulative
Players: 5
Age: 8–12
Equipment: 2 fir cones or small objects

FIGURE 4.29   At the same time . . .

➤➤**HOW TO PLAY**

Four players stand in a circle and pass the two fir cones around the circle. The fifth player, called the Warden, runs about twenty to thirty paces away from the other players, stops, and without looking back calls "Stop!" The circle player who is holding or about to receive the two fir cones runs to the Warden and gives him one of the cones. At the same time as the player leaves the circle with the two cones, the other circle players run and hide behind any available cover. The two cone holders try to find the hidden players. The player who finds the most hidden players becomes the new Warden.

➤➤PATTYWHACK

Country: Canada
Type: Manipulative
Players: 5
Age: 8–12
Equipment: 1 beanbag or ball

➤➤HOW TO PLAY

Four players assume a square formation with about three meters between players and begin to pass a beanbag in a counterclockwise direction. The fifth player stands a few yards away, with his back to the group, and whenever he feels like it, gives the signal, "Pattywhack!" The person who has the beanbag stays in his position until all other players are lined up behind player number five. Number five calls, "Ready!" and the player with the beanbag must crawl through the tunnel and receive a few gentle Pattywhacks on his behind.

FIGURE 4.30   Pattywhack

➤➤MERRY-GO-ROUND

Country: Germany
Type: Manipulative
Players: 5
Age: 8–12
Equipment: 1 skipping rope and 1 beanbag

➤➤HOW TO PLAY

The beanbag is tied to the end of the skipping rope. One player pulls the rope around him in a circular motion while the four other players must jump over it. The rope may be raised or lowered and moved faster or slower according to the wishes of the rope turner. If a person is touched by the rope, he replaces the player in the center.

FIGURE 4.31   Other players must jump . . .

➤➤BOKSTARSBOLL (LETTER BALL)

Country: Sweden
Type: Manipulative
Players: 4–5
Age: 7–9
Equipment: 2 hoops and
1 ball

➤➤HOW TO PLAY

FIGURE 4.32   The first player in the line

One child holds a hoop
in front of himself and
directly over another hoop on the ground. The other players line up behind a line
drawn two to three meters away from the hoop. The child holding the hoop thinks
of the name of an animal. He may, depending on the maturity of the players, give
some hints such as "It's small and white . . . and it flies." The first player in the line
tries to throw the ball into the upper hoop so it will land in the hoop on the floor.
If it lands inside the second hoop, he tries to guess the first letter of the animal's
name. If correct, he gets another try for the second letter, and so on. If he answers
incorrectly, the next player takes his turn. The game continues until a player spells
the full name of the animal.

➤➤DOUBLE OR NOTHING

Country: Zimbabwe
Type: Ball
Players: 4
Age: 7–10
Equipment: 2 cans and
2 small balls

➤➤HOW TO PLAY

Two players on team A
stand on a line and hold a
tin can with both hands.
The two opposing players
on team B stand on a line
five meters away and hold

FIGURE 4.33   Both players must catch the ball . . .

a small ball in their hands. The game begins with two players on team B simultaneously throwing the balls into the air and toward team A. Both players on team
A try to catch the balls in their tin cans. If both players are successful, team A gets
one point. If one or both players fail to catch the ball, they exchange positions with
team B. The first team to score five points wins the game.

➤➤JOGO DOTACO

Country: Brazil
Type: Ball
Players: 4
Age: 9–12
Equipment: 2 bats and 2 tin cans

➤➤HOW TO PLAY

Each team has a batter and a catcher. Two cans are placed about five meters apart. The catcher for each team stays behind a can and the batter just in front and to the side of it. The game begins with the catcher on team A throwing the ball toward team B's can. If he hits the can, he changes places with his partner. However, if the batter on team B hits the ball, batters on both teams run and touch their opponent's can with their bat, scoring one point, then return to their own can. Other runs can be attempted until the catcher on team A has recovered the ball and run back and touched his can. As soon as the can is touched, batters must return to their starting positions and the game continues until one team has scored ten points.

➤➤SHOO BALL

Country: Israel
Type: Manipulative
Players: 2
Age: 6–7
Equipment: 2 traffic cones, 4 sticks, and 1 ball

FIGURE 4.34 . . . and rolls the ball along . . .

➤➤HOW TO PLAY

Arrange equipment as shown in the photograph. The traffic cones are about one to three meters apart. Player A places a short stick in front and a long stick behind. Player B sits on the side and behind the halfway mark, then rolls the ball along the track towards his opponent's cone. Player A must keep the sticks in the holes as he tries to prevent player B from scoring. One point is scored for each ball that goes into the cone. Players change positions after each turn. The player who scores five points first wins the game.

➤➤PINBALL

Country: Denmark
Type: Ball
Players: 2
Age: 8–12
Equipment: 2 traffic cones and 1 tennis ball

➤➤HOW TO PLAY

Players stand about three meters apart and hold traffic cones with both hands. One player places a tennis ball in her cone and then scoops it toward her opponent. If the ball is caught in the cone, the game continues. If the ball is dropped, one Life is lost by the player who dropped it. A Life is also lost by the thrower if the ball is not thrown with an upward arc and over the center line between the two players.

FIGURE 4.35   If the ball is caught . . .

➤➤DANGEROUS CIRCLE

Country: Romania
Type: Ball
Players: 4
Age: 7–12
Equipment: 1 hoop and 2 ropes

➤➤HOW TO PLAY

Place two ropes (or draw a line) about ten meters apart and place a hoop in the center. Players on team A start behind their rope and players on team B must stay inside their hoop. Play begins with players on team A throwing the ball at team B. Players on team B try to catch the ball or dodge it. If a player catches the ball before it touches the ground, he remains in the hoop and must roll the ball to his opponent. However, if a player is hit, he changes places with the player who threw the ball.

➤➤DOUBLE THE FUN

Country: Czech Republic
Type: Ball
Players: 4
Age: 7–12
Equipment: 2 balls

➤➤HOW TO PLAY

Four players kneel and face each other in a square. Two players are given a ball. On a signal, the balls may be thrown to any player. However, two balls may not be thrown to the same player at the same time. When this occurs, the balls go back to the throwers and the game starts over. A player who misses or drops the ball is given one penalty point. The player with the least number of points wins the game. As skill increases, players can move farther apart and play with one-handed catches, using the right then the left hand.

➤➤SNATCHER

Country: Switzerland
Type: Ball
Players: 5
Age: 9–12
Equipment: ball

FIGURE 4.36   . . . two balls may not be thrown to . . .

➤➤HOW TO PLAY

Three players, A, B, and C, stand at an equal distance from each other. Player D tries to dribble the ball around the three standing players. Player E is the Snatcher and tries to take the ball away from player D or force him to drop it. If the Snatcher is successful, she takes player D's place. Player D exchanges places with player A, who, in turn, becomes the new Snatcher. The game continues until all players have had a turn at being the Snatcher.

FIGURE 4.37   . . . tries to dribble the ball around . . .

➤➤BEANBAG POLO

Country: Mexico
Type: Manipulative
Players: 4
Age: 9–12
Equipment: 2 boxes, 1 beanbag, 4 sticks

FIGURE 4.38   . . . or steal the beanbag away . . .

➤➤HOW TO PLAY

The beanbag is placed in the middle of the playing area. On a signal, two opposing players attempt to gain possession of the beanbag and pass it to a partner or try to shoot it into the opponent's box. Sticks must not be raised above the waist and may be used to pass, shoot, or strike an opponent's stick. One point is earned for each goal.

➤➤LOG ROLLER

Country: Russia
Type: Manipulative
Players: 2
Age: 9–12
Equipment: Balance beam or log

➤➤HOW TO PLAY

Two players stand on opposite ends of a log with their arms crossed and close to the body. On a signal, both players move toward the center and try to force the other off the log. There are several variations children enjoy playing. For example, holding their hands behind their backs, sideways, or overhead makes it more difficult for both players to maintain good balance. Also, sitting on the log, as well as changing leg and arm positions, provides additional challenges.

➤➤SHOOT THE SPINNING TOP

Country: Israel
Type: Ball

Players: 5
Age: 7–9
Equipment: 1 hoop and 4 balls

▶▶HOW TO PLAY

Four players form a circle and the fifth player stands in the middle with a hoop. Each circle player has a ball. On a signal, the middle player holds the hoop with outstretched arms and begins to turn in place. Circle players try to throw their balls through the hoop. The first player whose ball does not go through the hoop changes places with the player in the middle. Players receive one point every

FIGURE 4.39   Circle players try to throw the ball . . .

time their ball goes through the hoop, and the first player to accumulate ten points wins the game.

▶▶NAME THE ANIMAL

Country: Cuba
Type: Ball
Players: 4
Age: 7–10
Equipment: Ball and cards

▶▶HOW TO PLAY

Two teams, A and B, stand on two lines approximately three meters apart. Each team has a box of animal cards. A small blackboard or paper and pencil is located near the two teams. The game begins with one

FIGURE 4.40   . . . one player throws a small ball . . .

player on team A throwing the ball to either player on team B. If the player catches the ball, he writes his name on the blackboard. The player who threw the ball takes a card from his team's box and says the name of the animal written on it and asks his opponent, "Does it have hair?" If the answer is correct, player B gets one point for his team. If the player on team B fails to catch the ball, the player on team A who threw the ball writes her name on the blackboard and the player on team B must select a card from his team's box, say the name of the animal, and ask the same question. If the answer is correct, his team gets one point and the game continues. The first team to score 10 points wins the game.

➤➤➤Chapter Five

NEW GAMES FOR SIX TO FIFTEEN PLAYERS

In the previous chapter, challenges were limited to two to five players with simple rules and limited equipment. The new games in this chapter are the children's creative interpretations of more complex game challenges, involving more players and at times more equipment, skills, and rules.

When children are presented with a challenge that appears to be simple, they have to decide for themselves just how complicated their game should be. For example, the challenge "Can you make up a new tag game for ten to twelve players?" produced "One-Two-Three, Catch Me" (page 114). Another challenge with more rules, such as "Can you invent a game that has chasing in it? You must use a beanbag in your game and, at some time, you must throw it," resulted in the game called "Gold" (page 110). And a task requiring the use of a lot of equipment, such as "Is it possible to invent a game that has five players on each team, a mat, a ball, and a hoop?" showed children were capable of understanding the complexity of the task. Their new game incorporated skills learned in their game and gymnastic programs, in a constructive, safe, and imaginative way.

The other games in this chapter are the children's answers to individual challenges made up by their own teachers. The content of each challenge indicates that the teachers were becoming used to working with this exploratory method of teaching game activities. The game that resulted also revealed how well children adapted to new approaches to learning game skills and strategies. In turn, the games created by the children demonstrate the enthusiasm with which they embraced this new method. Their new games also incorporated previously learned material in a constructive, safe, and imaginative way.

➤➤**GOLD**

Country: England
Type: Ball

Name of Game	Country	Type	Players	Age	Equipment	Page
Gold	England	Ball	6–15	7–12	Beanbag	110
Ball in Boxes	England	Ball	6–15	7–12	Beanbag	111
Avoid the Circle	Wales	Tag	6–8	9–12	Ball	112
Checkmate	U.S.A.	Manipulative	7–9	7–9	Blindfold	113
Columbola	Peru	Ball	6	7–10	Ball	113
One-Two-Three, Catch Me	Luxembourg	Tag	5–6	9–12	None	114
Beats Me	England	Manipulative	10	8–12	Ball, hoop	114
An Eye	Poland	Ball	6–10	8–10	Ball	115
Blind Hen	Austria	Ball	10–14	9–12	Ball, shoes	115
Slipper Ball	Austria	Ball	10–14	9–12	Shoes, ball	116
Flying Saucers	Romania	Running	8	7–9	Hoops, rope	116
Fastest and Mostest	Czech Republic	Ball	3–9	7–9	Ball	117
Scoops	Canada	Ball	6–14	7–10	Scoops, balls	117
Petanca	Spain	Ball	6–8	8–12	Balls	117
Miss and Run	Switzerland	Ball	6–15	9–12	Ball, hoop	119
Chocolate	Poland	Manipulative	6–14	7–12	None	119
El Bosque Encantado	Mexico	Tag	10–15	7–9	None	119
Halli Hallo	Austria	Ball	7–8	7–12	Ball, hoop	120
Nose to Nose	Greece	Manipulative	6–15	7–9	Matchbox	121
Grab the Rag	Hungary	Tag	5–10	9–12	Stick, rag	121

Players: 6–15
Age: 7–12
Equipment: 1 beanbag

▶▶HOW TO PLAY

One player is given the beanbag (Gold), and begins to run anywhere within the playing area. All the other players begin to chase after and try to tag him before he throws the beanbag in any direction. If he is tagged while holding the beanbag, he is "killed" and must remain standing with legs apart until the end of the game. The player who tags him takes the Gold, runs off in another direction, and repeats the action. If a

FIGURE 5.1   . . . before he throws the beanbag . . .

player throws the Gold before being tagged and no other player is willing to pick it up, the player who threw it picks it up and throws it again. The game continues until two players remain and are declared the winners.

▶▶BALL IN BOXES

Country: Jamaica
Type: Ball

FIGURE 5.2   . . . throws the ball into the box . . .

Players: 8
Age: 7–10
Equipment: 4 balls and 4 boxes

➤➤HOW TO PLAY

The group is divided into four teams and each team has a Thrower and a Catcher. On a signal from the leader, the Thrower tries to throw the ball into the box held by the Catcher. The Catcher can help the Thrower by lowering and raising the box to catch the ball. As soon as the ball is caught, partners change positions and the game continues. The first team to score ten points wins the game.

➤➤AVOID THE CIRCLE

Country: Wales
Type: Tag
Players: 6–8
Age: 9–12
Equipment: 1 ball

➤➤HOW TO PLAY

One player is selected to be A and stands in the middle of the circle. All circle players are named B1, B2, B3, and so on to the last number.

FIGURE 5.3   Avoid the circle . . .

On the signal "Go," A tries to tag any circle player. Once a circle player is caught, she becomes known as C player and must go to the center of the circle. If C can bounce a ball five times in a row, she becomes a B player again. If she fails to bounce the ball the correct number of times, she becomes player A. The game starts over after a child successfully bounces the ball five times. If a player is caught a second time, she must hop on one foot while bouncing the ball. When caught the third time, she hops on one foot with eyes closed while bouncing the ball. Make up your own rules for a player caught the fourth or fifth time.

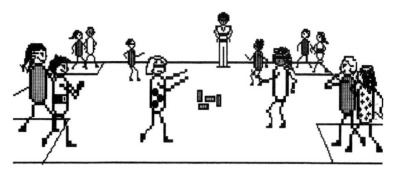

FIGURE 5.4   They use this method to guide

►►CHECKMATE

Country: United States
Type: Manipulative
Players: 7–9
Age: 7–9
Equipment: 4 blindfolds and 4 small objects

►►HOW TO PLAY

Divide the group into four teams and place four objects in the middle of the playing area. Blindfold one member of each team and have team members turn this person around three times. Each group decides on a method of communicating by sound that does not use words (such as clapping, hissing, or whistling). They then use this method to guide their blindfolded teammate to the center, to pick up an object, and to bring it back to the group. The first person back wins the game for his team.

►►COLUMBOLA

Country: Peru
Type: Ball
Players: 6
Age: 7–10
Equipment: 1 ball and 1 goal

►►HOW TO PLAY

Two teams line up on each side of a bench, facing the field of play. The leader throws the ball as far as possible and the first person on each

FIGURE 5.5   . . . and the first person on each . . .

team runs after it. The first person to pick it up gets a free throw at the goal while his opponent must stand still. If the ball goes through the goal, his team gets one point and the next players in line take their turn. If the ball does not go through the goal, both players run after it and continue the game until someone scores a goal.

➤➤ONE-TWO-THREE, CATCH ME

Country: Luxembourg
Type: Tag
Players: 5–6 on each team
Age: 9–12
Equipment: None

➤➤HOW TO PLAY

Arrange two teams of five to six players on opposite lines drawn about ten meters apart. Player number one from team A runs across to team B, who are standing behind their line with their hands stretched out to be tagged. Player number one must tap three hands then turn and run back across her own line. After the third tap, the whole opposing team runs after player number one. If she is tagged before reaching her own line, she becomes a prisoner and must stand behind the opposing team. If she makes it across her own line before being tagged, the last person tapped becomes her prisoner. Teams alternate turns and continue to the last player on each team. The team with the most prisoners wins the game.

➤➤BEATS ME

Country: England
Type: Manipulative
Players: 10
Age: 8–12
Equipment: 1 mat, 1 ball, and 1 hoop

➤➤HOW TO PLAY

Each team has five players, and each is designated as the Batting or the Fielding team. Each member of the Batting team is allowed one fair pitch before the teams

FIGURE 5.6   Beats me

exchange positions. The pitcher or bowler of the Fielding team throws the ball to the first batter. If the batter hits the ball, she performs a forward roll over the mat, runs around the hoop, and performs another forward roll. She must do these movements before the Fielding team can retrieve the ball and return it to the pitcher, who must remain inside the hoop. Teams exchange positions after the third batter has had her turn.

➤➤AN EYE

Country: Poland
Type: Ball
Players: 6–10
Age: 8–10
Equipment: 1 small ball

➤➤HOW TO PLAY

Draw a playing area as shown in the accompanying diagram. Players line up along the center line. The first player is given a ball and may choose to throw the ball into any geometrical area. Each player has his turn, then moves back to the next line and repeats the game. The game is repeated on the next line and the team with the highest score wins the game. The game can be played with different types of balls and requiring different types of throws, such as right- and left-hand throws and overhand and underhand throws.

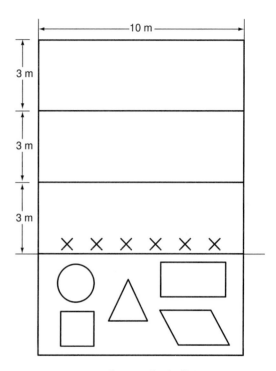

FIGURE 5.7 . . . throw the ball into any geometrical area . . .

➤➤BLIND HEN

Country: Spain
Type: Manipulative
Players: 10–14
Age: 9–12
Equipment: 1 blindfold

➤➤HOW TO PLAY

One player is blindfolded and all the other players must stay within the designated play area. On a signal, the blindfolded player tries to tag another player. When a player is tagged, he must

FIGURE 5.8 . . . tries to tag another player . . .

stop and remain motionless as the blindfolded player tries to feel and identify the player. If he guesses correctly, they change places and the game starts again. If not, the blindfolded player returns to the center and the game continues.

▶▶SLIPPER BALL

Country: Austria
Type: Ball
Players: 10–14
Age: 9–12
Equipment: Shoes and
a ball

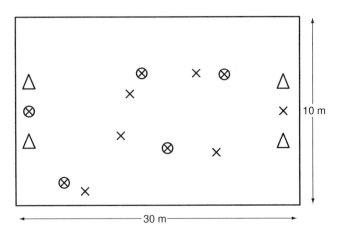

FIGURE 5.9   Playing Area

▶▶HOW TO PLAY

Mark off a playing area as shown in the diagram. Use a soft ball or make one out of crunched up paper and masking tape. The goalie places both shoes on his hands and all other players may use only one shoe. Players on each team may move anywhere with the playing area. The game begins with one Goalie rolling the ball to a teammate. Players can only use the hand holding the shoe to pass the ball or try to score a goal. The Goalie is the only player who can use both "hands" to pick the ball up and pass it to another player. One point is earned for each goal that is scored. The team with the highest number of points wins the game.

▶▶FLYING SAUCERS

Country: Romania
Type: Running
Players: 8
Age: 7–9
Equipment: Hoops and rope

FIGURE 5.10   Partners begin equal distance apart . . .

▶▶HOW TO PLAY

Make a large circle on the ground with skipping ropes. Partners begin an equal distance apart and stand inside their hoops and hold them about waist high. On a signal, Flying Saucers begin to run clockwise around Earth and try to pass as many other Flying Saucers as possible. One point is earned each time another Flying Saucer is passed, and the team with the highest score wins the game. To add additional challenges, have partners face opposite directions, have partners skip, hop, or move in another way as they progress around Earth.

➤➤THE FASTEST AND MOSTEST

Country: Czech Republic
Type: Ball
Players: 3–9
Age: 7–9
Equipment: Balls

➤➤HOW TO PLAY

Mark off three circles with a diameter of about .5 meter. Draw a line ten meters from the circles and place each team behind the line facing their own circle. In a time of one minute, each player tries to get his tennis ball into his circle as many times as possible. Each ball, however, must stop somewhere within the circle to count. After each player has thrown the third ball, and there is still time remaining, he may run, gather his balls, return to the starting line, and start throwing his balls back at his target. The game continues as many minutes as there are players and the team with the highest score wins the game.

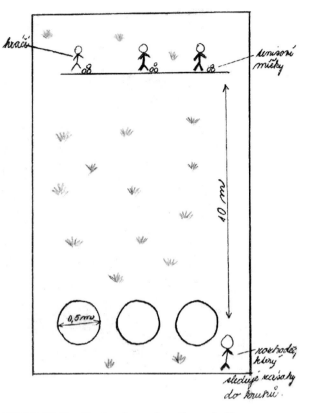

FIGURE 5.11   Each player has three balls

➤➤SCOOPS

Country: Canada
Type: Ball
Players: 6–14
Age: 7–10
Equipment: Scoops and a ball

➤➤HOW TO PLAY

Arrange each team on opposite sides of a fence (goalposts, for example). Each player has a scoop and may stand anywhere on his own side of the fence. One player places the ball in his scoop and then tosses it over the fence. If a player on the opposite team catches the ball in his scoop before it lands on the ground, his team gets one point. The team with the highest score wins the game.

➤➤PETANCA

Country: Spain
Type: Ball
Players: 6–8
Age: 8–12
Equipment: Balls

FIGURE 5.12   ... on opposite sides of the fence ...

▶▶HOW TO PLAY

Draw a rolling line and place a small ball about six meters in front of the line. Each player selects a number from a hat. The player with the lowest number tries to roll her ball as close to the small ball as possible. The player with the next lowest number takes his turn and so on until the last player. A player's ball may hit another player's ball or hit the small ball until the last player has had her turn. The player who ends up closest to the small ball at the end of the game wins.

FIGURE 5.13   Closest to the small ball wins ...

➤➤MISS AND RUN

Country: Switzerland
Type: Ball
Players: 6–15
Age: 9–12
Equipment: Ball and rope

➤➤HOW TO PLAY

Use a volleyball court (approximately 10 × 30 meters) and tie a rope across the two center posts. Each team lines up in two rows on their own side of the rope. Play begins with players on one team throwing the ball to a teammate. After the first or second pass, the ball must be thrown

FIGURE 5.14   . . . both teams must run and . . .

over the net. If a player on the opposing team catches the ball inside the court area and before it touches the floor, the game continues. If the ball is not caught, or dropped after catching it, or if it lands outside the playing area, players on both teams must run and stand inside their hoops (only three players per hoop). If the team that made an error reaches their hoop first, they receive one point. If the nonoffending team gets there first, they receive two points. The first team to score ten points wins the game.

➤➤CHOCOLATE

├── 1½' ──┤

TULIP	NARCISSUS
DAISY	ROSE
PANSY	PINK
VIOLET	LILY

FIGURE 5.15   Chocolate

Country: Poland
Type: Manipulative
Players: 6–14
Age: 7–12
Equipment: None

➤➤HOW TO PLAY

Draw a playing area as shown in the diagram. A player on one team starts the game by giving the first player on the other team a task, such as, "Call out the name of a flower on each square and hop on your left foot as you travel from square to square." If the player makes it all the way through the playing area without making a mistake, he gets one point and the right to present the next challenge to the next player. If a player makes a mistake, he goes to the end of the line and the next player takes his turn. Players may not use the same category as any previous player, and the player who reaches ten points first wins the game.

➤➤EL BOSQUE ENCANTADO

Country: Mexico
Type: Tag
Players: 10–15
Age: 7–9
Equipment: None

FIGURE 5.16   . . . by curling up into a small . . .

➤➤HOW TO PLAY

Draw a circle inside the playing area to be used as the Witch's Den. One player is chosen to be the Witch and all the other players scatter in the playing area. On a signal, everyone begins to run in different directions to avoid being tagged by the Witch. To avoid being tagged, a player may become a Tree by stopping and raising her hands overhead, or a Rock by curling up into a small ball. When a player is fairly tagged he must go to the Witch's Den and remain there until the end of the game. The last player to be tagged wins the game.

➤➤HALLI HALO

Country: Austria
Type: Ball
Players: 7–8
Age: 7–12
Equipment: Ball and hoop

FIGURE 5.17   . . . must throw the ball into a small . . .

➤➤HOW TO PLAY

One player is chosen to be It and stands in the middle of the circle of players. To start the game, the player in the center of the circle thinks of a word and then calls out the first letter as she throws the ball to a circle player. If the player who catches the ball does not guess the word, the ball is thrown back to the center player who throws it to another player and calls out the second letter of the word. When a player guesses the correct word, she throws the ball on the ground, signaling everyone to run away from It. It must retrieve the ball and then call "Stop," signaling everyone to stop immediately and stand still. Once It has possession of the ball, she may take as many steps as the guessed word has syllables toward any player. When It reaches the last step toward the chosen player, the chosen player must make a goal with her arms. If It can throw the ball through the player's arms, that player becomes It and the game is repeated. If It fails to be successful, she continues to be It and the game starts again.

➤➤NOSE TO NOSE

Country: Greece
Type: Manipulative
Players: 6–15
Age: 7–9
Equipment: 1 matchbox

FIGURE 5.18   . . . without using hands . . .

➤➤HOW TO PLAY

The group forms a circle and each player sits down in a cross-legged position. One player holds an empty matchbox on his nose, and then, without using her hands, tries to pass it to the next player. If a player uses any other part of her body, except the nose, or drops the matchbox, she is out of the game. The winners are the last two players holding the box between their noses.

➤➤GRAB THE RAG

Country: Hungary
Type: Tag
Players: 5–10
Age: 9–12
Equipment: 1 stick and 1 rag

➤➤**HOW TO PLAY**

Draw two lines about ten meters apart and place a stick in the middle with the rag on top. The two opposing teams line up on opposite lines. Each team secretly decides their order of running. When the leader calls out "One, Two, Three," the players from each team run out to the pole. As soon as a player grabs the rag, he must run back over his own end line. If the opposing players can tag the player with the rag before he gets back over the line, he must join the other team. If the player with the rag gets back before being tagged, he may choose one of the three opponents to become a new member of his team. The winner is the team with the largest number of players at the end of the game.

Chapter Six

NEW GAMES FOR SIXTEEN OR MORE PLAYERS

As the size of the group expands, the task of making up a game becomes increasingly difficult for young children. The tag games, such as "Hunter and Wolf" and "Tag Bag," were the result of a challenge that asked, "Can you invent a new tag game for the whole group and that only uses three sticks?" Each of the games invented from this single challenge were all different, showing how divergent each group of children can be when interpreting the same task. The games these children produced ranged from guessing, to making group statues, to a variety of manipulative games. All of which demonstrates that, given the freedom to design their own games, all children, regardless of cultural background, or any limitations in playing space or equipment, can create new games that are very creative and always enjoyable to play.

➤➤DRAGNET

Country: Zimbabwe
Type: Manipulative
Players: 16 or more
Age: 10–12
Equipment: None

FIGURE 6.1 animals try to break through

Name of Game	Country	Type	Players	Age	Equipment	Page
Dragnet	Zimbabwe	Manipulative	16 or more	7–10	None	123
The Statues	Greece	Manipulative	16 or more	7–10	None	125
Hunter and Wolf	Germany	Tag	16 or more	8–10	Hoops, sticks	125
Tag Bag	England	Tag	16 or more	7–12	Beanbags	126
Yo-Yo	Poland	Manipulative	16 or more	10–12	None	126
Detective	Austria	Guessing	16 or more	9–12	None	127
Magic Raygun	New Zealand	Tag	16 or more	9–12	Sticks	128
Three Sticks	Botswana	Tag	16 or more	8–10	Sticks	128
Friendly Knockout	Czech Republic	Ball	16 or more	8–12	Balls	129
Three Pin Tag	China	Tag	16 or more	9–12	Cones	129
Help	Scotland	Tag	16 or more	7–12	Sticks	130
Without Hands	Zimbabwe	Manipulative	16 or more	7–10	Stones	130
Stick Hunter	Sweden	Tag	16 or more	7–12	Sticks	131
Charge	Australia	Tag	16 or more	9–12	Sticks	132
Shoelace Catch	Austria	Manipulative	16 or more	9–12	Shoelaces	132
The Conductor	Romania	Guessing	16 or more	7–10	None	133
Scout Ball	Italy	Ball	16 or more	10–12	Balls, ribbons	133
Surround Tag	Japan	Tag	16 or more	8–12	Sticks	134
Headband Tag	Argentina	Tag	16 or more	8–10	Headbands	134
Go for It	U.S.A.	Tag	16 or more	8–12	Sticks	135
Stick Tag	Canada	Tag	16 or more	7–10	Sticks	135
Truck and Tractor	Romania	Tag	16 or more	8–10	None	135
Wizard	Peru	Tag	16 or more	8–12	Sticks	136
Anoo	Iran	Run	16 or more	10–12	None	137
Cold Winds	England	Tag	16 or more	7–10	Ribbons	137
Four Squares	Barbados	Ball	16 or more	10–12	Ball	138
One-Legged Fight	Nigeria	Manipulative	16 or more	10–12	None	139
Gallo Desplumado	Mexico	Manipulative	16 or more	9–12	Paper	139
Color Tag	Cuba	Tag	16 or more	9–12	None	140
Pair Tag	Greece	Tag	16 or more	7–12	None	140
Piggyback Polo	Botswana	Manipulative	16 or more	9–12	Ball	141
One, Two, Three Tag	Japan	Tag	16 or more	8–12	None	141
War	New Zealand	Ball	16 or more	9–12	Balls	142
Stolen Ball	Argentina	Ball	16 or more	10–12	Ball	142
Empire Strikes Back	Canada	Manipulative	16 or more	8–12	Balls	143
Chase Me	China	Tag	16 or more	8–12	None	143
Change the Spot	Australia	Tag	16 or more	8–12	None	144
Twirlies	Scotland	Manipulative	16 or more	7–9	None	145
Pole Handball	Canada	Ball	16 or more	10–12	Ball, backboard	145
Gates	Czech Republic	Tag	16 or more	8–12	None	146
Fire and Dynamite	Switzerland	Tag	16 or more	8–12	None	146
Coral Tag	Mexico	Tag	16 or more	8–12	None	147
Hog Ball	South Africa	Ball	16 or more	8–12	Balls, hoop	148

▶▶HOW TO PLAY

Divide the group into two equal teams and place each team behind two lines drawn about two meters apart. Team A joins hands and become the Hunters. Team B stands behind their own line without hands joined and become the Animals. The game starts with both teams moving cautiously toward each other. At any moment, the Animals try to break through the advancing Hunters. If an animal is pushed back to his own line, he is considered caught and joins the Hunters. Animals who push or break through to the opposite line are safe. All caught animals remain on the Hunters' team and the game is started over. The last Animal to be caught wins the game.

FIGURE 6.2 **"one, two, three."**

➤➤THE STATUES

Country: Greece
Type: Manipulative and tag
Players: 16 or more
Age: 7–10
Equipment: None

➤➤HOW TO PLAY

One player is selected to be It and stands facing a tree or wall. All other players stand about ten to fifteen meters away. It begins to count aloud from one to ten. As It counts, all other players move quickly toward him. When It stops counting, everyone must immediately stop and pretend they are statues. If any player moves, laughs, or speaks while It is looking at them, she must return to the starting line. It returns to counting and stopping, and so on, until another player touches him. As soon as It is touched, he runs after any player and tries to tag the player before she reaches the starting line. If the player is tagged, she becomes the next It and the game starts over. If not, It remains It.

➤➤HUNTER AND WOLF

Country: Germany
Type: Run and tag
Players: 16 or more
Age: 8–10
Equipment: 1 hoop, 3 sticks, and 3–4 small utility or Nerf balls

FIGURE 6.3 **If a wolf is hit . . .**

➤➤HOW TO PLAY

Divide the group into two teams. The Hunters guard the camp and the Wolves try to knock down the campfire (Sticks). If a Wolf is hit by a ball, he must sit down and not interfere with the game. The game ends when the last Wolf is seated or the campfire is knocked down. The teams change positions and start a new game.

FIGURE 6.4   Three players are chosen to be it . . .

➤➤TAG BAG

Country: England
Type: Tag
Players: 16 or more
Age: 7–12
Equipment: 3 beanbags and 3 hoops

➤➤HOW TO PLAY

One player takes three beanbags and throws them randomly inside the playing area. A hoop is placed around each beanbag. Three players are chosen to be It and pick up a beanbag. It players try to tag other players and, if successful, they give their beanbags to the new It and the game continues. During the game, each player has five Lives, which means she can go into the hoops (safe area) five times during the game.

➤➤YO-YO

Country: Poland
Type: Manipulative
Players: 16 or more
Age: 10–12
Equipment: None

➤➤HOW TO PLAY

Draw a playing area as shown in the accompanying diagram. The size of the area will depend on the available space and the age and number of children. The group is divided into teams A and B. They place themselves with three Guards in the area in front of the Treasure (use any small object for a Treasure) and the remaining players as shown in the diagram. On signal, each team starts moving toward the other team. When opposing players meet in the tunnel area, they must keep both feet on the ground and place their hands on each other's shoulders. When a player is pushed over any inside or outside line of the tunnel, he walks back to his original starting position. The winner keeps moving toward his opponent's Treasure. Players are not allowed to wrestle in the curved areas as they serve as resting places for both teams. The winner is the team to steal the Treasure.

▶▶DETECTIVE

Country: Austria
Type: Guessing
Players: 16 or more
Age: 9–12
Equipment: None

▶▶HOW TO PLAY

Players form a large circle and hold hands. One player is chosen to be the Detective and must move away from the group and cover her eyes and ears while the group selects the Murderer. The Detective then returns to the middle of the circle. The game begins with the Murderer secretly blinking at another circle player. The murdered player immediately sits down while all other circle players stare at the Detective. The Detective tries to identify the Murderer. The Murderer continues to blink and kill circle players until she is caught. The Detective and Murderer change places and repeat the game.

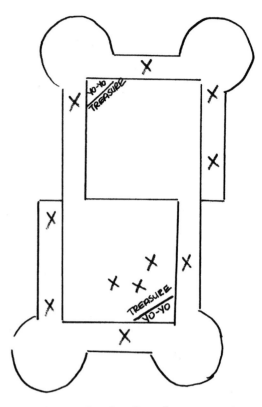

FIGURE 6.5   On signal, each team starts moving . . .

FIGURE 6.6   . . . secretly blinking at . . .

➤➤MAGIC RAYGUN

Country: New Zealand
Type: Tag
Players: 16 or more
Age: 9–12
Equipment: 3 sticks

FIGURE 6.7   . . . Since there are only three . . .

➤➤HOW TO PLAY

Divide the group into two equal teams and give each player on both teams a number. The teams begin on opposite ends of the field. Place the sticks in the circle located in the center of the field. The teacher calls out two numbers and the four children with these numbers run to the middle to retrieve the stick and become the Killers. Because there are only three sticks, one team has an advantage over the other on the basis of how many sticks they picked up. As soon as the Magic Rayguns are picked up, both teams run as fast as they can to the other end of the field. If a player with a gun tags an opponent, he must sit down where he was tagged. The team with the most players who reach the end line is the winner.

➤➤THREE STICKS

Country: Botswana
Type: Running
Players: 16 or more
Age: 8–10
Equipment: 3 sticks

FIGURE 6.8   . . . players run around the . . .

➤➤HOW TO PLAY

The class is divided into three equal teams and the first player of each team holds a stick. On the signal "Go," players run around the markers, which are about seven to ten meters away, and back to the next player. The first team to finish wins the relay.

➤➤FRIENDLY KNOCKOUT

Country: Czech Republic
Type: Ball and Tag
Players: 16 or more
Age: 8–12
Equipment: 2 balls

FIGURE 6.9   . . . tries to hit another player . . .

➤➤HOW TO PLAY

All the players are scattered in a designated playing area. The leader throws the balls into the area, signaling all players to try to grab one or both balls. As soon as a player has possession of a ball, she tries to hit another player with it. When a ball is thrown and does not hit another player, any player can pick it up after it has touched the ground. Any ball leaving the playing area can be retrieved by any player, but it cannot be thrown by this player until she has returned to the playing area. When a player is tagged, she must sit down. Any tagged player can be saved if a player with a ball throws it to her and she catches it in flight. Players try to get everyone else out or, for personal reasons, try to get some out and save others.

➤➤THREE PIN TAG

Country: China
Type: Tag
Players: 16 or more
Age: 9–12
Equipment: 3 traffic cones

➤➤HOW TO PLAY

Arrange three traffic cones about one to one-and-a-half meters apart. One child is chosen to be It and the remaining players must stay within the designated playing area. When a player is tagged by It, he becomes the new It and must run around the three traffic cones and back before he can try to tag another player. If the game is too slow, shorten the distance between each traffic cone or add two more Taggers.

➤➤HELP

Country: Scotland
Type: Tag
Players: 16 or more
Age: 7–12
Equipment: 3 sticks

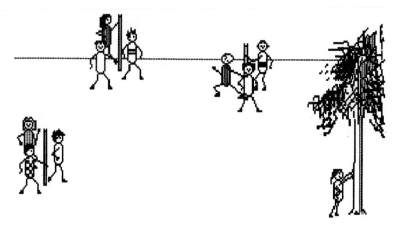

FIGURE 6.10   . . . When everyone is ready . . .

➤➤HOW TO PLAY

One player is chosen to be the Catcher. Three sticks are placed in the ground and numbered one, two, and three. The Catcher stands facing the tree or any suitable Home. All the other players select one stick and stand beside it. When everyone is ready, one of the players calls "Help." The Catcher calls a number, one, two, or three, and the players at that stick must run to another stick without being tagged. Any player who is caught joins the Catcher and helps catch the remaining players the next time around. The last player to be tagged wins the game.

➤➤WITHOUT HANDS

Country: Zimbabwe
Type: Manipulative
Players: 16 or more
Age: 7–10
Equipment: Stones

➤➤HOW TO PLAY

Players stand behind a line with a stone placed on any part of their bodies except, of course, their hands. On a signal, everyone races to a designated line. Once players start moving, they cannot touch their stones. Any player who touches or drops his stone must turn around three times, replace the stone, and continue the game. The first player to cross over the line wins the game. Repeat the game by adding another stone and selecting different parts of the body to balance them on.

FIGURE 6.11   . . . with a stone placed on . . .

➤➤STICK HUNTER

Country: Sweden
Type: Tag
Players: 16 or more
Age: 7–12
Equipment: 3 sticks

➤➤HOW TO PLAY

Three sticks are given to three children. One of the remaining players who does not have a stick is chosen to be the Hunter. On a signal from the teacher, the Hunter tries to tag another player. Any player who holds a stick cannot be tagged and, when a player is about to be tagged, she can be saved if one of the stick holders hands her a stick. However, only one person at a time is allowed to hold a stick. When a player is fairly tagged, she becomes the new Hunter and calls out, "I am the new Hunter," before she can chase another player.

FIGURE 6.12   . . . when a player is about to . . .

▶▶CHARGE

Country: Australia
Type: Tag
Players: 16 or more
Age: 9–12
Equipment: 3 sticks

FIGURE 6.13   . . . who may charge at any time . . .

▶▶HOW TO PLAY

Two players are chosen to be the Guards of the sticks (Treasure), which are placed on the ground one yard inside the boundary line (to allow players to go behind them). The two Guards try to prevent the sticks from being captured by the other players, who may charge at any time to get the sticks. Charging players, however, can only run and dodge while trying to grab the sticks; they cannot touch the Guards. A Guard may leave his post to tag a player who has picked up a stick. If the Guard tags the player, that player is out of the game unless she has reached Home Fort on the other side of the playing area. When a player is caught, the stick is returned to the original position for another "charge." The game is over when the Treasure (three sticks) has been successfully stolen.

▶▶SHOELACE CATCH

Country: Austria
Type: Manipulative
Players: 16 or more
Age: 9–12
Equipment: Shoelaces

▶▶HOW TO PLAY

Choose a small playing area (free of obstacles), such as a classroom or draw a playing square

FIGURE 6.14   As soon as another player is . . .

outside. All players should have laces in their shoes; if not, they carry a small piece of rope. Two players are selected to be It and tie their inside shoes together. When ready, It tries to tag another player. As soon as another player is tagged, he ties his shoelace with the outside shoe of one of the two taggers. The game continues and the last two players remaining become the new Its for the next game.

➤➤THE CONDUCTOR

Country: Romania
Type: Guessing
Players: 16 or more
Age: 7–10
Equipment: None

➤➤HOW TO PLAY

The group is arranged as an orchestra and is taught how to mime playing different instruments (accordion, guitar, piano, drums, etc.). One player is chosen to be the Spectator and stands in front of the Orchestra and facing away. While facing away, another player is selected to be the Conductor and remains in her own place. The Conductor begins playing an instrument, such as the drums, and everyone begins to copy her. The Spectator is told to turn around and guess who is playing the Conductor. As the game continues, the Conductor quietly changes to another instrument until she is caught. As soon as the Conductor is caught, a new Conductor and Spectator are chosen and the game is repeated.

➤➤SCOUT BALL

Country: Italy
Type: Ball
Players: 16 or more
Age: 10–12
Equipment: Ribbons, 1 ball, and 2 goals

FIGURE 6.15   When a player has the ball . . .

➤➤HOW TO PLAY

Divide the group into two teams. All players tuck a ribbon into the back of their shorts. Scout ball is played on an open field, with goals set at either end. A player can take five steps with the ball, then she must pass it to a teammate. The object is to carry the ball through the Goalposts. The opponents try to intercept the ball as it is being passed from player to player. When a player has the ball, she can be "scalped," that is, lose the colored ribbon tucked into her shorts. When this happens, the ball goes to the nearest opponent and the scalped player runs to her own goal, touches it, then replaces her ribbon and rejoins the game. One point is awarded each time the attacking team can move the ball through their opponent's Goal.

▶▶SURROUND TAG

Country: Japan
Type: Tag
Players: 16 or more
Age: 8–12
Equipment: 3 sticks

▶▶HOW TO PLAY

Three players are chosen to be the Taggers and each is given a stick. All other players must stay within the designated playing area. The three Taggers try to surround a player. When a player is surrounded by three players, he exchanges positions with

FIGURE 6.16   When a player is surrounded . . .

one of the Taggers. The method of selecting which one of the Taggers to exchange positions with is decided by the following procedure: The tagged player thinks of a number between one and ten and the Tagger who guesses closest to the number changes positions.

▶▶HEADBAND TAG

Country: Argentina
Type: Tag
Players: 16 or more
Age: 8–10
Equipment: Red and yellow bands

FIGURE 6.17   . . . players begin to run anywhere . . .

▶▶HOW TO PLAY

Two Taggers are selected and each is given a headband to wear (yellow or red). The rest of the class are Runners. In each of the four corners of the playing area are bags containing yellow and red headbands. On a signal from the teacher, players begin to run anywhere in the designated playing area. When a player is tagged, he runs to the corner and picks up a headband that is the color of the player who tagged him. He then puts the headband on and becomes another Tagger. The game ends when everyone is wearing a headband, and the Tagger who gathered the most headbands is the winner.

▶▶GO FOR IT

Country: United States
Type: Tag
Players: 16 or more
Age: 8–12
Equipment: 3 sticks

▶▶HOW TO PLAY

The group is divided into four equal teams. All players of each team sit down except the first player in each line. On a signal, the first players race to pick up a stick

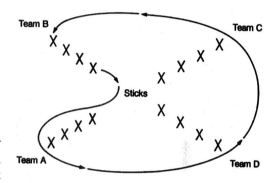

FIGURE 6.18   Go for it

from the center of the playing area. After picking up the stick, the players run in the same direction around the outside of the four teams (counterclockwise), replace the stick in the center, return to the end of their team's line, and sit down. When they complete this, they receive one point for their team. A player who does not pick up a stick must run in the same direction and try to tag a player who has a stick. If he tags one of these players, the tagged player must give him his stick and walk to the end of his own team. Play continues until everyone has had a turn, and the team with the highest number of points wins the game.

▶▶STICK TAG

Country: Canada
Type: Tag
Players: 16 or more
Age: 7–10
Equipment: 3 sticks about 6 to 8 feet long and 3 to 5 ribbons

▶▶HOW TO PLAY

Three sticks are randomly placed in the designated playing area and three to five players are chosen to be Taggers. Taggers wear ribbons and begin to chase other players. A player is safe when she is balancing on one foot on the stick. Any number of players may balance on the stick and remain as long as they like, providing they maintain the one-foot balance position.

▶▶TRUCK AND TRAILER

Country: Romania
Type: Tag

FIGURE 6.19   A player is safe when . . .

Players: 16 or more
Age: 8–10
Equipment: None

►►HOW TO PLAY

Draw a playing area about ten meters square and signal players to find a place in the area. Two players are chosen to be a Truck and a Trailer. The Trailer gets behind the Truck and holds on to her waist. On a signal the Truck and Trailer try to tag another player. When a player is tagged, he becomes another Truck

FIGURE 6.20   . . . try to tag another player . . .

and tries to tag another player to become his Trailer. Trucks and Trailers keep chasing other players until the last player is caught.

►►WIZARD

Country: Peru
Type: Tag
Players: 16 or more
Age: 8–12
Equipment: 3 sticks

►►HOW TO PLAY

One player is chosen to be the Wizard and stands in the middle of the playing area with three sticks. All the other players must scatter in the playing area. The Wizard calls

FIGURE 6.21   As soon as a player . . .

out "one, two, three," then begins to chase after the players. As soon as a player is touched with a stick, she must take it and become another Wizard. The game continues for a few minutes, then a new Wizard is chosen and given the three sticks to begin the game.

▶▶ANOO

Country: Iran
Type: Running
Players: 16 or more
Age: 10–12
Equipment: None

FIGURE 6.22   . . . without taking a breath . . .

▶▶HOW TO PLAY

The group forms a large circle and one player is chosen to be It. It must run around the circle and back to his spot without taking a breath. Each player, in turn, takes his turn. All players who make it around without taking a breath are Winners. Those who did not make it without taking a breath are declared the Losers and must piggyback another player a specified distance and back. (*Anoo* is an Arabic word that means "a loud and rough voice or cry.")

▶▶COLD WINDS

Country: England
Type: Tag
Players: 16 or more
Age: 7–10
Equipment: 3 colored ribbons

▶▶HOW TO PLAY

Three players are chosen to be the Taggers and stand in the middle of the playing area. They tuck a colored ribbon in their shorts. All the other players scatter in the playing area. On a signal from the leader, the Taggers try to tag as many players as possible. When a player is tagged, she must stand still and hold her hands above her head. Tagged players can be rescued if another player can circle her before

FIGURE 6.23   . . . and hold her hands . . .

being tagged. The game continues until all players are standing with their hands above their heads.

►►FOUR SQUARES

Country: Barbados
Type: Ball
Players: 16 or more
Age: 10–12
Equipment: 1 large ball

►►HOW TO PLAY

The class is divided into four teams with two players from each team assigned to guard their own home square (two meters by two meters). The diagonally opposite home square is each team's opponent's home square. Players from any team may scatter anywhere they wish in the playing area. The game is started with a jump ball between four opposing players. A point is scored every time a ball touches an opponent's home square. After a point is scored, a player on the defending team throws the ball into play from his home square.

FIGURE 6.24   The game is started with a . . .

➤➤ONE-LEGGED FIGHT

Country: Nigeria
Type: Manipulative
Players: 16 or more
Age: 10–12
Equipment: None

FIGURE 6.25   . . . try to make an opponent . . .

➤➤HOW TO PLAY

Arrange the players into two equal teams. Each team starts on a line facing their opponent's team, about three meters away. Players on both teams hold their arms across their chest and grasp their own elbows. On a signal, players keep their arms folded and hop on one foot toward their opponents. One or more players on one team try to make an opponent lose his balance and touch his other foot to the ground. Once a player loses his balance, he must return to his own line until the end of the game. The winner is the team with the most players who remain standing at the end of the game.

➤➤GALLO DESPLUMADO

Country: Mexico
Type: Manipulative
Players: 16 or more
Age: 9–12
Equipment: Paper strips

➤➤HOW TO PLAY

Every player ties three to five pieces of crepe paper (½ meter in length) on each arm. On a signal, players must keep their arms away from their body while they try to remove paper strips from the arms of other players. The winner is the one who has the most strips on her arm at the end of the game.

FIGURE 6.26   . . . then try to remove . . .

➤➤COLOR TAG

Country: Cuba
Type: Tag
Players: 16 or more
Age: 9–12
Equipment: None

➤➤HOW TO PLAY

Draw a playing area according to the available space and age of children. Everyone, except two children scatter in the playing area. The two chosen players stand with their backs to the other children and call out a color, such as "Purple." They turn around and try to tag any player with

FIGURE 6.27   . . . by moving and hiding them . . .

that color on any part of their shoes, clothing, or hair. Players who do not have that color on may try to help their teammates from being tagged by moving and hiding them or moving in front of the oncoming tagger. However, they cannot touch the oncoming tagger. When two players are tagged, they exchange positions and the game starts over with a new color.

➤➤PAIR TAG

Country: Greece
Type: Tag
Players: 16 or more
Age: 7–12
Equipment: None

➤➤HOW TO PLAY

One player is chosen to be the Hunter. All the other players form pairs, hold hands, and stand in their own circle marked on the ground. Each pair calls out or is given the name of an animal. When the Hunter calls the name of one or more

FIGURE 6.28   When the hunter calls the . . .

animals, pairs with those names must keep holding hands, run around three other circles, and back to their own circle. If the Hunter tags a pair before they return to their circle, they are out of the game. The last pair remaining in the game is declared the winner.

➤➤PIGGYBACK POLO

Country: Botswana
Type: Manipulative and ball
Players: 16 or more
Age: 9–12
Equipment: 1 ball

FIGURE 6.29   Players on the outside circle . . .

➤➤HOW TO PLAY

The group is divided into partners of equal size and weight. Partners then form a double circle with one child in the middle holding a ball. Players on the outside circle jump onto their partner's back. When everyone is ready, the player in the center throws the ball to any mounted player. Mounted players continue throwing the ball to any other mounted player. When a player makes a poor throw or drops the ball, he changes position with the player in the middle. Before the new middle player throws the ball, all the pairs reverse positions.

➤➤ONE, TWO, THREE TAG

Country: Japan
Type: Tag
Players: 16 or more
Age: 8–12
Equipment: None

➤➤HOW TO PLAY

Four circles are drawn near the four corners of the playing area and one in the middle. Place four Taggers in the center circle and place equal numbers of players in

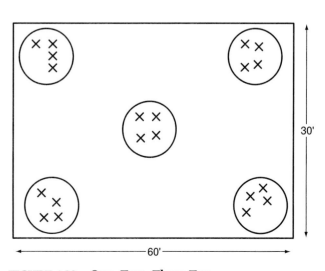

FIGURE 6.30   One, Two, Three Tag

the outer circles. One Tagger in the center circle is designated to give a whistle command, one of three, that all four groups must follow:

1. One whistle: All groups move to the next circle on their right.
2. Two whistles: All groups move to the next circle on their left.
3. Three whistles: All groups remain in their own circles.

On the first two commands, Taggers try to tag the players before they reach the next circle. If a player moves out of his present circle on three whistles, he moves to the center circle and becomes a Tagger. After five or six signals, the outer circle with the most players wins the game.

▶▶WAR

Country: New Zealand
Type: Ball
Players: 16 or more
Age: 9–12
Equipment: 15 utility balls

FIGURE 6.31   **On a signal from the teacher . . .**

▶▶HOW TO PLAY

Divide the group into two teams and assign each a home area. Place fifteen utility balls on the center line. On a signal from the leader, any number of players from each team may rush forward and pick up one or more balls. The object of the game is to hit an opponent below the waist with a ball. A player can be hit while in any part of the playing area. However, attacking players cannot advance beyond the opponent's home base line. When a player is fairly hit, he must stand on the side or end line and may pass the ball to his teammates but may not throw the ball at an opponent. Any player may retrieve a ball that has gone out-of-bounds but must always throw it to a teammate.

▶▶STOLEN BALL

Country: Argentina
Type: Ball and tag
Players: 16 or more
Age: 10–12
Equipment: 1 ball

▶▶HOW TO PLAY

Divide the group into two equal teams and arrange each team as shown in the illustration. One ball is placed in each goal. A Safety Zone is marked three yards in front of each goal and parallel to the center line. The aim of the game is for each team to steal their opponent's ball and bring it back to their own Safety Zone. Players on each team cannot be tagged in their own half of the field. When a player crosses the center line and is tagged before she reaches her opponent's Safety Zone, she must remain in place until another "untouched" teammate tags her

FIGURE 6.32   If a player reaches her opponent . . .

free. If a player reaches her opponent's Safety Zone, she cannot be tagged while remaining in this area. This player, and any other teammate who is in the opponent's Safety Zone, may pick up the ball and try to run back across to her own half of the field without being tagged. These players may pass the ball back and forth as they run through their opponent's half of the field. However, if they are tagged or drop the ball, they must stay where they were tagged and the ball is returned to their opponent's goal. One point is scored for each successfully stolen ball. The game starts over after each point is scored.

▶▶EMPIRE STRIKES BACK

Country: Canada
Type: Manipulative
Players: 16 or more
Age: 8–12
Equipment: Hoops and utility balls

▶▶HOW TO PLAY

The players are scattered throughout the playing area. Everyone except It has a hoop that he holds around his waist and uses as a spaceship. These people are the Forces of Evil and It belongs to the Good Side. It has a utility ball that he kicks, trying to hit the Forces of Evil, who are flying about in their Spaceships. Players who are the Forces of Evil who are hit with a ball then trade in their hoop for a ball and become members of the Good Side. The game ends when all the Forces of Evil players are caught.

▶▶CHASE ME

Country: China
Type: Tag
Players: 16 or more
Age: 8–12
Equipment: None

▶▶HOW TO PLAY

The group is arranged into partners who stand one behind the other, scattered throughout the playing area. One player is selected to be It. Another player is chosen to be the Runner, who stands behind any set of partners. On a signal, the

FIGURE 6.33   . . . the Runners try to . . .

Runner tries to run and stand in front of another group while the It tries to tag her. If the Runner is tagged before she reaches her target, she exchanges places with It and the game continues in the same manner. If the Runner successfully reaches her target, the player at the rear of this set of partners becomes the new Runner and must start to run to the front of a new set with It now trying to tag her.

➤➤CHANGE THE SPOT

Country: Australia
Type: Tag
Players: 16 or more
Age: 8–12
Equipment: None

FIGURE 6.34   . . . Change to a hop . . .

➤➤HOW TO PLAY

Mark off a playing area about twenty yards square. One player is chosen to be It and all the other players scatter in the playing area. It picks three danger marks on the floor and tells the teacher where they are located. The remainder of the class does not know where these danger spots are. The game begins with a signal from It such as "Run forward." As the players are moving, It may direct them to change directions or to change to a hop, run, or slide, and so forth. When a person steps on or crosses over the first danger spot, It calls that person's name, and that player must stop, call out his own name, then continue moving. It may continue to use the first danger spot or if she notices the class avoiding the spot, she will call out "Number two spot!" and continue changing locomotor movements and directions. The game continues until It has used her three danger spots and cannot catch any players.

▶▶TWIRLIES

Country: Scotland
Type: Manipulative and tag
Players: 16 or more
Age: 7–9
Equipment: None

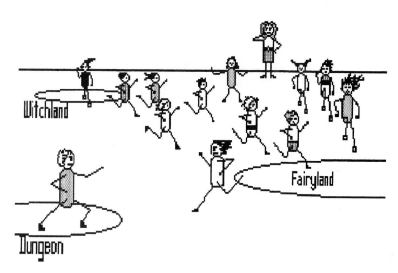

FIGURE 6.35   . . . If the "Fairy Queen" can run . . .

▶▶HOW TO PLAY

Witchland, Fairyland, and the Dungeon are marked on the ground as shown in the illustration. One player is chosen to be the Witch (tagger) and another to be the Fairy Queen. The other players start twirling around near the center of the playing area with their eyes closed. As they twirl in place, the teacher calls Home, signaling the players to keep their eyes closed but to stop twirling and begin to walk forward. As soon as a player walks toward Witchland, the Witch must call out, "Open your eyes," signaling all the players to open their eyes and run for Fairyland. If a player is tagged before reaching Fairyland, she goes to the Dungeon. If the Fairy Queen can run to the Dungeon and touch a tagged player before the Witch tags her, both players have safe passage back to Fairyland. However, if the Fairy Queen is tagged by the Witch before she can touch a tagged player, they exchange positions and the game starts over.

▶▶POLE HANDBALL

Country: Canada
Type: Ball
Players: 16 or more
Age: 10–12
Equipment: 1 ball, backboard, and 2 cones

▶▶HOW TO PLAY

Divide the group into two equal teams. If there are more than twelve players per side, half of each team is designated as court players and the other half as sideline players. The game begins with a jump ball at the center of the court. Players may

FIGURE 6.36   The game begins with . . .

advance the ball only by throwing it; dribbling with hands or kicking the ball is not allowed. Players must also pass the ball within three seconds of receiving it. A goal is scored if the ball hits any part of the basketball backboard superstructure. The goalie may attempt to prevent the ball from hitting the structure. If playing inside a gymnasium, the ball is still in play if it hits the wall. Any foul, such as unnecessary roughness, traveling, or time violation, is penalized by a penalty shot from the center of the court. The penalty shot must be taken by a player who has not scored, and the goalie may not defend the goal during a penalty shot. A sideline player may not score but may receive and pass the ball to a sideline or court player. Sideline players rotate with court players every two minutes.

▶▶GATES

Country: Czech Republic
Type: Tag
Players: 16 or more
Age: 8–10
Equipment: None

▶▶HOW TO PLAY

The group is arranged in partners who find a place in the playing area, join hands, and form a Bridge. The Bridge may be tall or low but, once decided, must remain in that position. One player is chosen to be It and another the Chaser. On a signal, It starts to run and pass through the gates. A few seconds later, the Chaser starts to chase It. The Chaser must follow Its pathway until she tags It. When this occurs, a new It and Chaser are chosen for the next game.

▶▶FIRE AND DYNAMITE

Country: Switzerland
Type: Tag
Players: 16 or more
Age: 8–12
Equipment: None

FIGURE 6.38   When a player is tagged . . .

FIGURE 6.37   . . . it starts to run . . .

➤➤HOW TO PLAY

Two players are selected to be Catchers. One Catcher wears a yellow band (Fire), the other wears red (Dynamite). If a yellow Catcher tags a player, she is not eliminated until tagged by a red Catcher (or vice versa). A player who is tagged more than once by the same Catcher stays in the game until tagged by both colors. When a player is tagged by both Catchers, she must wait on the sideline until another player is caught. When this occurs, the two tagged players become the new red and yellow Catchers and the game continues.

➤➤CORAL TAG

Country: Mexico
Type: Tag
Players: 16 or more
Age: 8–12
Equipment: None

➤➤HOW TO PLAY

Mark off a playing area, and divide the group into two equal teams. Each team selects two players to be Horses. The Horses join hands while their other teammates join hands and form a circle around the Horses. On a signal, both teams release their Horses who, in turn, must keep their hands joined as they try not to be captured by the opposing team. The opposing team must keep their hands joined and try to circle and capture the other team's Horse. The first team to capture a Horse wins the game.

FIGURE 6.39   . . . must keep hands joined . . .

➤➤HOG BALL

Country: South Africa
Type: Ball
Players: 16 or more
Age: 8–12
Equipment: Balls, hoops

➤➤HOW TO PLAY

Arrange the playing area as shown in the diagram. Player number one from each team runs and gets the ball from the center of the circle, returns, and stands three meters away from her team, then passes the ball to each player on her team. From here, the player runs to her end line and bounces the ball in her team's hoop, then returns to the center and places the ball into her team's other hoop. She then runs and tags player number two who repeats the same movements. The first team to complete the relay wins the game.

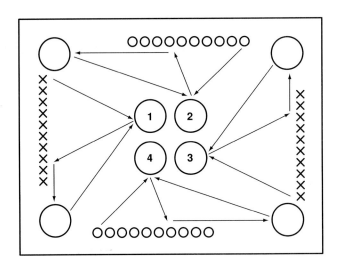

FIGURE 6.40   Hog Ball

►►►Chapter Seven

HOW TO HELP CHILDREN CREATE THEIR OWN GAMES

Young children usually learn to play running, tag, and simple ball games by playing with older children, through instructional programs in school, or in recreational settings. Games, such as poison tag, dodgeball, and marbles, are taught to children according to fixed rules and playing space. There are no variations in the game unless the instructor or the children agree to them prior to starting the game. For these reasons, abruptly asking them to create their own games may cause some initial problems. To provide a transition or bridge to this new approach, instructors should begin with a game the children know and enjoy, then gradually show how they can change the activity to make it more challenging and enjoyable. The discussion of Dodgeball illustrates how to start with a game children already know, then begin to change it in a gradual and enjoyable manner.

►►CHANGING THE RULES OF DODGEBALL

In this situation, the instructor has organized the group into two teams to play Dodgeball (Chapter 2, page 40). The game is played for a few minutes, then the instructor asks the group to stop and listen. The instructor uses the following four elements to introduce a change in the game.

Elements of the Game of Dodgeball
1. **Number of Players:** Class is divided into two equal groups
2. **Playing Space:** A large circle
3. **Skills and Rules:** Throwing and hitting below the waist
4. **Equipment:** Two inflated balls

FIGURE 7.1   The game is played for a few minutes

The instructor decides to pose a challenge that will vary the **skills and rules.**

> When you start the next game, players in the center must hop on one foot at all times, and circle players can only throw the ball backward through their legs.

After a few minutes, she stops the game and tells all the original circle players to sit down in one corner of the playing area, and the original center players in another corner. She mentions to the group that she changed the rules of their game and now is going to give them an opportunity to do the same. She says: "Each team has one minute to think up a new rule for the game."

After the minute is up, they return to the game with the center players explaining their new rule, which usually will be a rule that applies to the circle players. Then the circle players explain their rule and the game begins. After a few minutes, the process is repeated, keeping the previous new rules and adding two more. Continue this procedure a few times then try it with another game the children like to play.

FIGURE 7.2   . . . through their legs . . .

FIGURE 7.3   The new rule is . . .

The process of introducing creative games has begun. The tools are the four elements **(1) players, (2) space, (3) skills and rules, and (4) equipment** through which the teacher or children can impose limitations or changes. This procedure should be repeated with other games, such as Partner Tag, Crab Soccer, or Keep Away. When the children feel comfortable with the idea and results of changing their favorite games, try the Creative Games Approach described below.

▶▶CREATIVE GAMES APPROACH

The Creative Games Approach entails posing tasks or challenges to children that involve the four elements of a game outlined in the accompanying chart. These four elements are used as a simple grid to develop a series of challenges. It is suggested that instructors begin this approach by posing a very simple challenge, such as the one described below. Each successful challenge should include all four elements with a gradual increase in the number of players, playing space, pieces of equipment, and complexity of skills and rules. The accompanying situation and the four challenges will provide a format for instructors to start using this approach. Instructors should adapt challenges to meet the needs and interests of their students.

Creative Games Chart

Number of Players	Playing Space	Equipment	Skills and Rules
From individual activities	From limited space	From use of simple equipment	From single skills and rules
To	To	To	To
Partner activities	Use of more space	Use of more varied and complex equipment	Use of more complex skills and rules
To			
Group activities			

Situation: Twenty-eight children, age seven and eight.

Sets of small equipment, such as hoops, traffic cones, balls, and individual ropes.

Playing space: outdoors on blacktop area.

FIGURE 7.4 . . . turn
around and catch it . . .

▶▶CHALLENGE NUMBER ONE

Give every child a utility ball and then tell them to find their own space in the
playing area. When the children are ready, pose the following challenge: "See if
you can stay in your own space and make up a game that you can play by your-
self. Your game must have a throw and a catch."

> Name of Game: Bounce and Turn
> Description of Game:
> First you bounce the ball with one hand then you turn around and catch it before
> it touches the floor.—Matthew, age 8

As the children are developing their own game, walk around the group and
occasionally say "Remember your game must have a throw and a catch," "Try to
stay in your own space," or provide other verbal cues. Also, praise the children as
they create ideas, such as turning around in place as the ball is thrown in the air
or bouncing and catching the ball. It is important to remember that once children
have begun to create their own games, instructors should not interfere in this
process by imposing their own ideas into the children's games. Also, do not try to
anticipate what type of game each child or group will invent. If children are given
freedom to create, they will produce original and exciting games.

After several minutes, ask everyone to stop and sit down with the ball. Select
one or two children to demonstrate their game to the group, then move to the
next challenge.

FIGURE 7.5 . . . you try
to keep the ball . . .

▶▶CHALLENGE NUMBER TWO

Give every child a ball and a hoop, then pose the following challenge: "Can you
invent a new game using your ball and hoop?"

> Name of Game: Twirl and Spin
> Description of Game:
> I put the hoop around my waist and start spinning the rope. Then I twirled the ball
> on my finger. One or two people can play. The first person to drop the ball or hoop
> loses. If you play by yourself, you try to keep the ball on your finger while spinning
> the hoop.—Alex, age 8

According to the Creative Games Chart, the challenge is limited to one
player, but new equipment has been added, and the player must stay in his own
space or move anywhere in the playing space. Repeat the same procedure while
walking through the group, reminding the children of the elements and praising
them for their creative ideas. Select a few children to demonstrate their games,
then move on to the next challenge.

▶▶CHALLENGE NUMBER THREE

Refer to the Creative Games Chart. This challenge could stay with the individual
player (give her more space, and increase the number and complexity of equipment, skills, and rules), but it will increase the number of players. Here, the group
is arranged in partners who have one ball and two traffic cones between them. The
third challenge is: "Invent a game with your partner that will use one ball, two
traffic cones, and dribbling the ball with your feet."

> Name of Game: Forming an Eight
> Description of Game:
> You need two cones, a ball, and two or more people. You put the cones at least two
> meters across from each other. Form a line and the first person puts the ball on top

FIGURE 7.6   . . . and make a figure of eight . . .

of the cone and then drops the ball. You kick the ball and dribble and make a figure of eight around the cones. You keep on doing this until someone messes up. That person is out who messes up. You keep doing this until one person is left. That person wins.—Angela, Joo, and Carissa, all age 8

Just before each set of partners begins to plan their game, add the following new rule:

Player A suggests the first rule of the game, player B adds the second rule, and so on, until you have jointly planned the game.

This challenge requires children to work together in the planning and playing of the game. If one child is overly aggressive, she will, in most cases, plan the whole game, while the less aggressive child will listen then passively play the game. Imposing the requirement that each player take his or her turn in the planning phase guarantees that both children have a share in the creation of the game. The result of this process is that both children will enjoy the game far more than if one child dominated the planning and playing of the game. Follow the same procedure used in the previous challenge and have one or two pairs demonstrate their game to the group.

▶▶CHALLENGE NUMBER FOUR

The next step is to present a challenge to groups of three or four children. To capitalize on the previous working relationships, have the same partners join up with other partners to form groups of four. Tell the new groups of four to return two traffic cones and one ball to their containers. Limiting the equipment to one ball and two traffic cones per group of four players will challenge their collective abilities, and perhaps produce a game that will be different from the obvious situation with two teams trying to throw or kick the ball through their opponent's goal. The following challenge should result in the invention of a novel game:

See if your group of four can make up a game using one ball and two traffic cones in your own space. Your game must include passing the ball with your feet, and everyone must be moving.

Name of Game: Diamond Ball
Description of Game:
Diamond Ball is a fun, fast game that includes a ball, two cones, and four players. The positions are a goalie, right wing, left wing, and a back player. The right and left wing pass to each other and try to score. If they score, the back player gets the ball

FIGURE 7.7   . . . and try to score . . .

and then they rotate from back to goalie, to left wing, to right wing, to the back player. So gather up three of your friends and play some Diamond Ball.—Ian Fraser, Peter Stiles, Isaac Cathers, and Jan Jones, All age 8

This challenge is open enough to allow the group to create a game of two versus two, or a new game in which each player will contribute to a single team effort. Providing only two rather than four traffic cones will encourage a group effort in whatever game is eventually created. Finally, the requirement that all players must always be moving adds to the general complexity and fun of the game.

Once the instructor has begun this process of encouraging children to create their own games, she should observe the children's behavior and make adjustments in the type of challenges, the time allowed to practice, and the way in which she encourages children to share their ideas. Generally speaking, after two or three challenges, the tone and creativity of the group will begin to flourish. From this point on use the Creative Games Chart as a grid to develop a sequence of challenges for the class.

➤➤➤Part Three

NEW COOPERATIVE GAMES CREATED BY CHILDREN

**Chapter Eight: New Cooperative Games for Two
to Five Players**
**Chapter Nine: New Cooperative Games for Six
to Fifteen Players**
**Chapter Ten: New Cooperative Games for Sixteen
or More Players**
**Chapter Eleven: How to Help Children Invent
Their Own Cooperative Games**

One dominant characteristic of the games children invented in Part Two was the competitive nature of their games. They inevitably came up with a game that had a winner and a loser. This observation applied to virtually every country and every age group. The question is: Is the creation of such games due to a competitive instinct all children are supposed to possess, or the result of the competitive model provided for them by adults? I believe the problem lies with the adult model. The games in Part Three demonstrate the potentially cooperative nature of children as well as the cooperative games they enjoy playing.

In order to help children create games that were noncompetitive, the teachers first taught their students the meaning of cooperative behavior. This was accomplished by having them play existing cooperative games that included the key elements of cooperation, fun, participation, equality, success, and trust. To illustrate, children were taught the game "Juggle a Number" (page 176), which required five players to keep five balls moving around the group at the same time. To accomplish this task, every player had to cooperate and trust his teammates to do the same if personal and group success were to be realized. Discussions followed after the game to make sure everyone understood the meaning and importance of these elements. Each key element was taught to the children in this manner. (See Chapter 11 for a detailed explanation of this process.)

When the teachers felt the children could work together toward a common goal, they began to present a series of game challenges that included one or more of the cooperative elements. For example, a challenge, such as "In your group of four, make up a game with one ball, one goal, and using your feet to move the ball. Your game must also show cooperation and trust." As the next three chapters demonstrate, this type of challenge was readily met by children from all parts of the world, resulting in games that possessed two or more cooperative elements.

Reactions from teachers who presented these challenges were interesting and generally positive. From Brazil: "A great number of children considered it difficult. Only after some time, after being engaged in such activity, they showed more interest in it. After being used to it they appreciated it very much." From Zimbabwe: "I think this approach stimulates more participation by students." And from Austria: "It helps children develop social behavior and become members of a group." Reactions from the students were also favorable: "Super. Wish we could do this more often" (Austria); "This method helps us get better ideas from our friends by working in groups and to be more creative" (Zimbabwe); and "It was very interesting because we could create our own games and choose what we wanted to do as opposed to other classes" (Brazil).

The cooperative games described in the next three chapters follow the same process as Part Two. Chapter 8 works with groups of two to five players, followed by six to fifteen players in Chapter 9, and, finally, with larger groups of sixteen or more children in Chapter 10. These games demonstrate that children, regardless of age or cultural background, can invent cooperative games that are exciting, safe, and enjoyable to play. Chapter 11 provides a description of the elements of a cooperative game, a step-by-step procedure for teaching these elements to children, and a series of challenges for small and large groups of children.

Chapter Eight

NEW COOPERATIVE GAMES FOR TWO TO FIVE PLAYERS

The games in this chapter for two players were the result of a challenge, "Can you design a cooperative game with your partner, using any available equipment? Your game must stress that each player has an equal role in the game and must, in some way, place trust in the other player." Children from around the world understood the concept and came up with interesting games. The two Japanese children who invented "Stick Exchange" (page 160) clearly showed they understood the meaning of trust and, of course, both have an equal role to play in the game. Other games, like "Double Tug" (South Africa, page 160), "Balance Challenge" (New Zealand, page 160), and "Blind Horse" (Germany, page 163), emphasize the elements of trust, equality, and, at times, other elements such as participation, cooperation, and success. The series of games for three came from the challenge, "See if your group of three can make up a game with one ball, one goal, and dribbling the ball with your feet. Your game must stress participation and success." The first part of this challenge is fairly structured: specifying one ball and one goal and the action of dribbling the ball with the feet. With these criteria it would be usual to invent a game that sets each player against the other with quick elimination and an early declared winner. However, the requirements of the challenge stated in the second sentence ensure that no player is eliminated, and that each player reaps some success through participating in the game. The few games requiring four or five players are the children's responses to special challenges some of the teachers designed and presented to their classes.

Name of Game	Country	Type	Players	Age	Equipment	Page
Under Ball	Botswana	Ball	2	8–10	Ball	158
Jump Hoop	England	Manipulative	2	7–10	Rope, hoop	158
Fingertips	Germany	Manipulative	2	8–12	Small equipment	159
Stick Exchange	Japan	Manipulative	2	8–12	Sticks	160
Double Tug	South Africa	Manipulative	2	8–12	Beanbags, hoops	160
Balance Challenge	New Zealand	Manipulative	2	8–12	Cones, planks	160
Ball Thrower	France	Ball	2	9–12	Bat, ball	161
Polo	Argentina	Manipulative	2	9–12	Ball, cones	161
Leap Ball	Australia	Ball	2	10–12	Ball, hoop	162
Hoop Scotch	Canada	Manipulative	2	8–12	Hoops	162
Blind Horse	Germany	Manipulative	2	10–12	Ropes	163
Blind Ball	Belgium	Ball	2	9–12	Ball	163
Two Noses	Luxembourg	Manipulative	2	7–12	Box, ball	164
Circle Catch	U.S.A.	Ball	2	8–12	Balls	164
Wall Catch	England	Ball	2	7–12	Ball	165
Changing Positions	Canada	Manipulative	2	7–9	Hoop, bench	165
Under the Leg	China	Ball	3	8–12	Ball	166
Three Boys	Botswana	Ball	3	8–12	Ball	166
Circle Goal	Jamica	Ball	3	9–12	Ball	167
Beanbag Smash	South Africa	Ball	3	8–10	Ball, beanbag	167
Snabbmal	Sweden	Ball	3	8–12	Ball	168
Claudia Berni	Italy	Ball	3	9–12	Ball, hoop	168
ABC Dribble	England	Ball	3	9–12	Ball, cones	169
Hoop Soccer	Australia	Ball	3	8–12	Hoop, basket	169
Firefighter Rescue	Canada	Ball	3	9–12	Ball, basket	170
Blind Horseman	Argentina	Ball	3	8–12	Ball, stick	170
Soapbox Soccer	U.S.A.	Ball	3	9–12	Ball, basket	171
Soccer circuit	New Zealand	Ball	3	9–12	Ball, cones	171
Triple Dribble	India	Ball	3	9–12	Ball, cone	172
Seesaw	Australia	Manipulative	3	10–12	None	172
Jump Ball	Botswana	Ball	3	8–10	Ball	173
Passing in the Square	Israel	Ball	4	7–9	Balls, balloons	173
Ting, Ting, Ting	Mexico	Manipulative	4	7–12	Lids	174
Backside Throw	Greece	Ball	5	7–9	Ball	174
Jumping the Hoop	Canada	Manipulative	2	7–10	Hoop, beanbag	175
Tin Can Toss	Mexico	Manipulative	5	8–10	Ball, can	175

▶▶UNDER BALL

Country: Botswana
Type: Ball
Players: 2
Age: 8–10
Equipment: 1 ball

▶▶HOW TO PLAY

One player stands with her legs apart while the other stands behind her with a ball. The player with the ball tries to bounce it between

FIGURE 8.1   tries to bounce the ball between . . .

her partner's legs so she can catch it as it bounces up through her legs. The game continues with each player taking a turn bouncing and then catching the ball.

▶▶JUMP HOOP

Country: England
Type: Manipulative

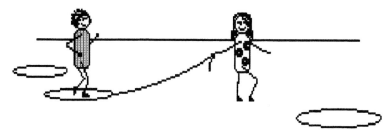

FIGURE 8.2   . . . as player "B" drags it across . . .

Players: 2
Age: 7–10
Equipment: 1 rope and 3 hoops

➤➤HOW TO PLAY

Place two hoops on the playing field about six meters apart. Player A stands in one hoop, and player B drags a second hoop, attached to a short rope, alongside of player A. The aim of the game is for player A to jump into player B's hoop and remain inside this hoop as player B drags it across to the third hoop. This is accomplished by player A taking short steps or jumps as player B pulls the hoop toward the third hoop. Players change positions and repeat action back to the first hoop.

➤➤FINGERTIPS

Country: Germany
Type: Manipulative
Players: 2
Age: 8–12
Equipment: Any available small equipment

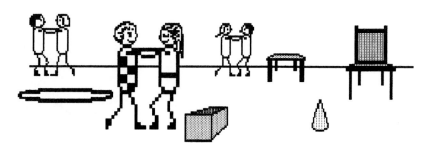

FIGURE 8.3   . . . they guide each other around . . .

➤➤HOW TO PLAY

A series of obstacles such as boxes, hoops, and benches are scattered around the playing area. The class is organized into partners who stand randomly throughout the playing area, facing each other. Partners lift their hands to shoulder level and lightly touch each other's shoulders. Now, without talking or using any other cues except through their fingertips, they guide each other around the obstacles by applying a little pressure through their fingers to let each other know whether they want to move forward, backward, right, left, up, or down. Game can continue in this fashion or with one partner keeping his eyes closed as they move throughout the obstacles.

➤➤STICK EXCHANGE

Country: Japan
Type: Manipulative
Players: 2
Age: 8–12
Equipment: 2 sticks, each approximately one meter in length

➤➤HOW TO PLAY

Two players assume a crawling position and face each other. One player places a stick on his right shoulder while the other places

FIGURE 8.4   Without using their hands . . .

the other end on his left shoulder. Without using their hands, they try to help each other move the stick to their other shoulder while gradually shifting to a standing position. After reaching a standing position, they try to reverse directions and return the stick to its original position. If either player uses his hands or if the stick drops off either player's shoulder, they must start from the beginning.

➤➤DOUBLE TUG

Country: South Africa
Type: Manipulative
Players: 2
Age: 8–12
Equipment: 2 beanbags and 1 hoop

➤➤HOW TO PLAY

Two beanbags are placed in the middle of the hoop. Players pair off and stand inside the hoop, facing each other and holding hands. They bend down and, using their partner's handhold for mutual support, lean backwards, and hold this position. When in this position, they reach forward and pick up a beanbag

FIGURE 8.5   . . . facing each other and holding . . .

with their free hand, then return the beanbag to the middle of their hoop. The action is repeated with the players adding elements to the game, such as placing the beanbag on their head or any other part of their body.

►►BALANCE CHALLENGE

Country: New Zealand
Type: Manipulative
Players: 2
Age: 9–12
Equipment: 2 traffic cones (skittles),
1 plank, and 1 block of wood

►►HOW TO PLAY

Arrange the equipment as shown in the illustration. Two players begin at the

FIGURE 8.6   . . . as they walk to opposite ends . . .

center of the plank and must keep the plank off the floor as they walk to opposite ends, pick up the skittle, and return to the starting position. If they are successful, the next challenge is to repeat the activity while each partner is balancing a beanbag on his or her head or throwing a ball back and forth as they move to the end and back.

►►BALL THROWER

Country: France
Type: Ball
Players: 2
Age: 9–12
Equipment: 1 bat, 1 tennis or sponge ball, and 6 skittles or bowling pins

►►HOW TO PLAY

The equipment is arranged as shown in the illustration. Player A bounces the ball toward player B. Player B tries to bat the ball and knock

FIGURE 8.7   . . . bounces the ball toward player B . . .

over as many skittles as possible. Players change positions after each throw. The challenge in this game is to try, as a pair, to knock all the skittles over with the fewest number of throws.

►►POLO

Country: Argentina
Type: Manipulative
Players: 2
Age: 9–12
Equipment: 1 ball, 6 traffic cones, and 1 long stick

FIGURE 8.8   The "Horse" carries the "Rider"

►►HOW TO PLAY

One player is designated as the Horse and the other as the Rider. The Horse carries the Rider from the starting line to the end line. The Rider has a long stick in his hand that he uses to push the ball between the traffic cones. If he knocks a traffic cone over, either by his stick or the ball, he must reset it. This is accomplished by joint effort; the Rider stays on the Horse and the Horse bends down so the Rider can reach the traffic cone and reset it while still mounted. Players exchange positions at the end line and repeat the activity back to the starting line.

►►LEAP BALL

Country: Australia
Type: Ball
Players: 2
Age: 10–12
Equipment: 1 ball and 1 hoop

FIGURE 8.9   **Player one begins in a leapfrog . . .**

►►HOW TO PLAY

Two hoops are placed on the ground about ten meters apart. Player one begins in a leapfrog position and player two rolls the ball through her legs, then leapfrogs over her. Player one repeats this action and so on, until they reach the opposite hoop. After reaching the hoop, one player begins to bounce the ball and, when the ball rebounds, the other partner makes the second bounce. Players keep alternating the bouncing movement until they return to the first hoop.

►►HOOPSCOTCH

Country: Canada
Type: Manipulative
Players: 2
Age: 8–12
Equipment: 9 hoops or circles drawn in dirt area

►►HOW TO PLAY

The two players first arrange their hoops as shown in the drawing. Players then begin one behind the other, starting out with hands on the waist of the one in front, and facing hoops one and two. They jump together, both landing with one foot in each hoop. The players jump again, placing both feet in hoop three.

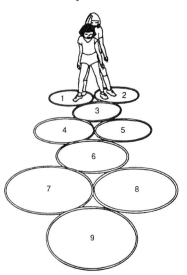

FIGURE 8.10   **Players then begin one behind the other . . .**

Next, they jump and place one foot each in hoops four and five, and both their feet in hoop six. The next jump results with one foot each in hoops seven and eight. The last jump is into hoop nine, where both players land with both feet in the hoop. Players turn around and repeat the same movements back to the starting position.

➤➤BLIND HORSE

Country: Germany
Type: Manipulative
Players: 2
Age: 10–12
Equipment: 1 skipping rope, small equipment

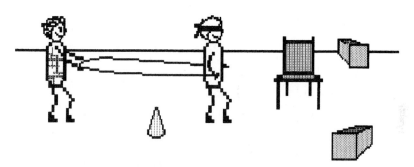

FIGURE 8.11   . . . and direct the "Horse" through . . .

➤➤HOW TO PLAY

One child is blindfolded and holds the ends of the skipping rope at his sides. The other player is the Driver and directs the Horse through a series of obstacles scattered around the playing area by gently pulling on the rope. The positions are changed every thirty seconds or whatever time schedule has been agreed on by the two players.

➤➤BLIND BALL

Country: Belgium
Type: Ball
Players: 2
Age: 9–12
Equipment: 1 ball

FIGURE 8.12   . . . stops then gives a verbal clue . . .

▶▶HOW TO PLAY

Two players stand about ten to twelve feet apart. Player A is blindfolded and holds the ball. Player B moves in any direction she wishes, stops, then gives a verbal clue to indicate where she is located. Player A throws the ball to player B, who tries to catch it without moving her feet. Players exchange positions after each throw and, if successful, extend the distance on each successive throw, and change the clue to a clap or short whistle.

▶▶TWO NOSES

Country: Luxembourg
Type: Manipulative
Players: 2
Age: 7–12
Equipment: 1 small box or small ball and 1 long skipping rope

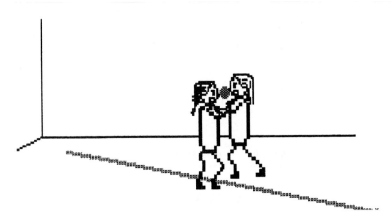

FIGURE 8.13 . . . **across the rope between their . . .**

▶▶HOW TO PLAY

A long rope is placed in a straight line on the floor. Two players stand on either side of the rope and hold a small object, such as a matchbox or Nerf ball, across the rope and between their noses. The aim of the players is to stay on their own side of the rope and follow its path without dropping the object. If successful, the next attempts should vary the position of the rope so that it curves, makes right angles, or whatever shape the two players decide to challenge.

▶▶CIRCLE CATCH

Country: United States
Type: Ball
Players: 2
Age: 8–10
Equipment: 2 balls

▶▶HOW TO PLAY

Players stand about six to seven feet apart, each holding a ball. On a signal from one of the players, both

FIGURE 8.14 . . . **each holding a ball . . .**

throw their ball toward the other. If both players catch the ball, they jump one step sideways in a counterclockwise direction, slightly turning as they do so in order to move in the shape of a circle with a diameter of two to three meters. However, if the ball is dropped, no matter how far they have progressed around the imaginary circle, they must return to the starting position. The object of this game is to complete the circle.

➤➤WALL CATCH

Country: England
Type: Ball
Players: 2
Age: 7–12
Equipment: 1 ball

FIGURE 8.15   If the other player catches it before . . .

➤➤HOW TO PLAY

The playing area is set up as shown in the drawing. The game starts with the pair standing behind the first line and one of the players throws the ball at the circle on the wall. If the other player catches it before it touches the ground, they receive one point. Partners exchange positions after every throw. The game is played to ten points, then the players move back to the next line and repeat the game until they have progressed to the line furthest from the wall.

➤➤CHANGING POSITIONS

Country: Canada
Type: Manipulative
Players: 2
Age: 7–9
Equipment: Hoops and a balance bench

➤➤HOW TO PLAY

Two players begin at either end of a balance bench, each holding a hoop around himself. They walk to the middle of the bench and, without losing their balance, pass each other and continue on to the opposite end. Once this has been completed successfully, the complexity of the game is increased by the players choosing a modification to the activity, such as balancing a beanbag on their heads or changing the method of moving to a hop, slide, or other movement.

➤➤UNDER THE LEG

Country: China
Type: Ball
Players: 3
Age: 8–12
Equipment: 1 ball

FIGURE 8.16   . . . under her right and left leg . . .

➤➤HOW TO PLAY

Players A, B, and C line up one behind the other with player A at the back of the line. Player A bounces the ball under her right and left leg and then rolls it through player B's legs. Player B repeats the same action, then rolls the ball through player C's legs. When player C gets the ball, she bounces it under each leg, then places it on the ground and kicks it into a box located about three meters away. Player C runs and retrieves the ball, takes it to the back of player A, and starts to bounce the ball under her right and then her left leg. After each player has had a turn, players may add new movements and rules.

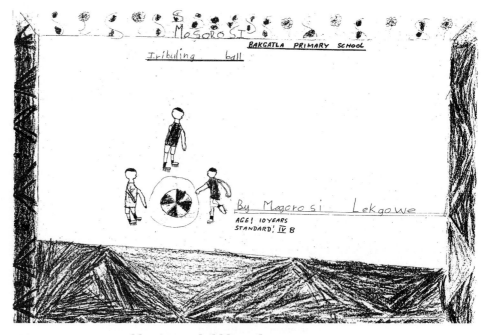

FIGURE 8.17   . . . and begins to dribble and pass . . .

➤➤THREE BOYS

Country: Botswana
Type: Ball

Players: 3
Age: 8–12
Equipment: 1 ball

➤➤HOW TO PLAY

A shallow hole, a box, or a hoop is used as a goal. Three players begin about six meters from the goal and begin to dribble and pass the ball to each other as they approach the goal. Any player can attempt to score providing he is at least two meters away from the goal. One point is awarded for each goal. The next player to attempt a goal must be one of the other two players. The game continues until the group has scored six points.

➤➤CIRCLE GOAL

Country: Jamaica
Type: Ball
Players: 3
Age: 9–12
Equipment: 1 soccer ball

FIGURE 8.18   Player "C" retreives the ball . . .

➤➤HOW TO PLAY

Arrange the playing area as shown in the illustration. Player A dribbles to B and remains there while player B dribbles to player C's position. Player B remains and player C dribbles toward the goal and, without crossing the shooting line, attempts to score a goal. Player C retrieves her ball, passes it to player B, then runs to take player A's old position. Players B and C repeat the same movements after each player rotates one position counterclockwise.

➤➤BEANBAG SMASH

Country: South Africa
Type: Ball
Players: 3
Age: 8–10
Equipment: 1 ball, 3 beanbags, and 3 traffic cones

➤➤HOW TO PLAY

Three beanbags are placed on top of a traffic cone. Three players then make a triangle shape around the traffic cone. The object of the game is to use any part of their bodies, except their hands, to move the ball so that it knocks the beanbags off the traffic cone. Players must always remain at least one meter away from the traffic cone.

FIGURE 8.19   The object of the game . . .

➤➤SNABBMAL (INSTANT GOAL)

Country: Sweden
Type: Ball
Players: 3
Age: 8–12
Equipment: 1 soccer ball

➤➤HOW TO PLAY

Three players begin dribbling and passing the ball to each other. Suddenly, player A moves away from the other two and spreads his legs to make a goal. The other two players must dribble and pass the ball at least two times before one of them tries to kick the ball between player A's legs. The game continues with players B and C taking their turn at making a goal.

FIGURE 8.20   . . . must dribble and pass the ball . . .

➤➤CLAUDIA BERNI

Country: Italy
Type: Ball
Players: 3
Age: 9–12
Equipment: 1 soccer ball and 1 hoop for each group of 3, and 8–12 traffic cones

FIGURE 8.21   If a group touches either obstacle . . .

►►HOW TO PLAY

Divide the class into groups of three and give each group one ball and one hoop. Two goals are marked on each end of the playground and the traffic cones are scattered throughout the playing area. Each group begins on one end line standing inside their hoop and holding it about waist high. The object of this game is for each group to dribble their ball around two traffic cones as they move toward the opposite end, then kick the ball and hit the post. If a group touches a traffic cone, they must pick up their ball, walk back to the starting line, and try again. No scores are kept and the membership of each group is changed every few minutes.

►►ABC DRIBBLE

Country: England
Type: Ball
Players: 3
Age: 9–12
Equipment: 1 soccer ball and 3 traffic cones

►►HOW TO PLAY

FIGURE 8.22   Player "A" dribbles around the . . .

Arrange players as shown in the diagram. Player A dribbles around the three traffic cones, shoots for a goal, then takes player B's position. If B stops the ball, she moves to player A's position and takes her turn. If player B fails to stop the ball, player C picks it up and runs to take player A's starting position. Player B drops back to player C's position and player A becomes the new goalkeeper. No score is kept, with all the players moving as fast as possible from one position to the next.

►►HOOP SOCCER

Country: Australia
Type: Ball
Players: 3
Age: 8–12
Equipment: 1 soccer ball, 1 hoop, and 1 basket

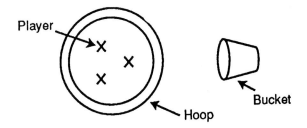

►►HOW TO PLAY

FIGURE 8.23   Three players stand inside the hoop . . .

Three players stand inside a hoop and hold it about waist high. Once inside the hoop, the players begin to dribble the ball toward the overturned basket. When they reach shooting distance, one player attempts to score a goal. They retrieve the ball and return to the starting line and start a new game. On the second attempt, a new player must attempt to shoot a goal. This procedure is followed on each successive attempt on the goal.

Note: Players found the most efficient way to dribble the ball was to rotate their positions within the hoop while moving toward the target. This movement allowed each player to touch the ball during the dribbling part of the game.

➤➤FIREFIGHTER'S RESCUE

Country: Canada
Type: Ball
Players: 3
Age: 9–12
Equipment: 1 ball and 1 basket

FIGURE 8.24   . . . the firefighters carry her back . . .

➤➤HOW TO PLAY

There are three players. Two form a firefighter's chair with their arms crossed and their hands joined, and the third player sits on their hands. A basket is placed on one side of the gymnasium as the starting point. When ready, the two firefighters carry the third player and begin to dribble and pass the ball toward the opposite side of the gymnasium. When they reach the other side, the third player picks up the ball between her feet, then the firefighters carry her back to the basket. The players rotate positions and repeat the game.

FIGURE 8.25   . . . the third player picks up the ball

➤➤BLIND HORSEMAN

Country: Argentina
Type: Ball
Players: 3
Age: 8–12
Equipment: 1 ball, 4 sticks, and 2 traffic cones

➤➤HOW TO PLAY

Arrange the playing area as shown in the illustration. Player A bends forward and puts his arms around player B's waist. Player C then sits on player A's back. Players A and B keep their eyes closed and player C guides them to move the ball

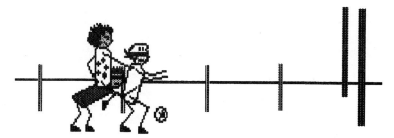

FIGURE 8.26   . . . and player "C" guides them . . .

around the four sticks and through the goal. Players change positions after each goal and begin at the starting line.

➤➤SOAPBOX SOCCER

Country: United States
Type: Ball
Players: 3
Age: 9–12
Equipment: 1 soccer ball and 1 basket

FIGURE 8.27   They must keep the ball inside . . .

➤➤HOW TO PLAY

A soccer ball is placed on the starting line. Three players hold hands and form a triangle around the ball. They must keep the ball inside the triangle and dribble the ball to the basket. When they reach the basket, each player can use one foot to help lift the ball into the basket. To repeat the game, players rotate clockwise as they dribble the ball toward the basket.

➤➤SOCCER CIRCUIT

Country: New Zealand
Type: Ball
Players: 3
Age: 9–12
Equipment: 1 ball and 2 traffic cones

➤➤HOW TO PLAY

Arrange players as shown in the illustration. Player A dribbles the ball around the goal. When he is at the side of the goal, he passes the ball to player B. As player B

receives the ball and at-
tempts to score a goal,
player A moves behind
the goal to stop the ball
if it gets past player C.
After player B takes his
turn, he takes player A's
original position, player
C becomes the new
shooter, and player A
becomes the goalkeeper.
The players rotate play-
ing positions to repeat
the game.

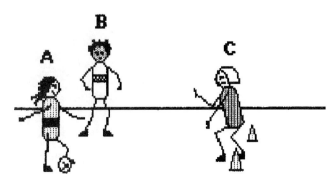

FIGURE 8.28   Player "A" dribbles the ball around . . .

►►TRIPLE DRIBBLE

Country: India
Type: Ball
Players: 3
Age: 9–12
Equipment: 1 ball and
2 traffic cones

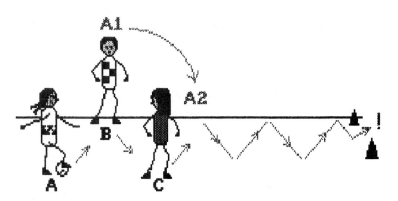

FIGURE 8.29   Player "A" dribbles the ball to . . .

►►HOW TO PLAY

Arrange players as shown in the illustration. Player A dribbles the ball to player B.
Player B then dribbles it to player C, while player A moves to a new position.
Player C now dribbles to player A while player B moves to a new position. The
rotation continues until one player can dribble the ball through the goal. The
game is repeated by starting from the original starting position.

►►SEESAW

Country: Australia
Type: Manipulative
Players: 3
Age: 10–12
Equipment: None

➤➤HOW TO PLAY

This is a game of trust that requires close supervision. Arrange the class into groups of three. The smallest and lightest of the three players stands between the other two players, and keeps his body as rigid as possible. When ready, the middle player, with his eyes closed, begins to fall toward an outside player. The outside player catches the player and gently pushes him toward the other player. Outside players continue to move the middle player back and forth for a few minutes.

FIGURE 8.30   . . . begins to fall forward . . .

➤➤JUMP BALL

Country: Botswana
Type: Ball
Players: 3
Age: 8–10
Equipment: 1 ball

➤➤HOW TO PLAY

Three players begin in a straight line with player A holding the ball. Player A bounces the ball to player C then changes positions with player B. Player C bounces the ball to player B and changes positions with player A. The rotation continues until someone commits an error; then the game can be started over.

FIGURE 8.31   . . . Player "A" bounces the ball to "C" . . .

➤➤PASSING IN THE SQUARE

Country: Israel
Type: Ball
Players: 4
Age: 7–9
Equipment: Balls or balloons; plastic strips

➤➤HOW TO PLAY

The children build a square with the four plastic strips. Each player stands on one corner holding a balloon or nylon ball. Player Number 1 calls out the name of another player and throws her ball up into the center of the square. The child whose name was called must quickly call another player's name, throw her balloon into the center, then try to catch player Number

FIGURE 8.32   . . . and throws the ball up . . .

1's ball. If a ball is dropped or goes out of reach, everyone stops and returns to their starting position. The game continues until all four names are called out. Player Number 2 begins the next game.

▶▶TING, TING, TING

Country: Mexico
Type: Manipulative
Players: 4
Age: 7–12

FIGURE 8.33   . . . throwing or sliding their lids . . .

Equipment: Lids of bottles

▶▶HOW TO PLAY

Draw a playing square with the four "Xs" in the middle. Players may stand or squat in their corners. They take turns throwing or sliding their lids so that they land on all or part of an X. Once each player has had a turn, and providing there are still lids that have not landed on an X, the player that is closer to any remaining lid retrieves it and throws or slides it toward any remaining X. The game continues until the last X is covered.

▶▶BACKSIDE THROW

Country: Greece
Type: Ball
Players: 5
Equipment: Ball

▶▶HOW TO PLAY

Five players are numbered from 1 to 5, and then scatter in a designated playing area. Player Number 1 has a ball and dribbles it five times while moving in any direction. After the fifth bounce, the player must hold the ball behind her back and throw it to player Number 2. If the ball does not go to player Number 2, any other player may pick it up but must pass it back to player Number 1 using the behind the back throw. The game continues until player Number 5 receives the ball. The

FIGURE 8.34   . . . then throws it to . . .

game is repeated with the ball passed backward through the legs, and the next game is played with another different way of throwing the ball.

►►JUMPING THE HOOP

Country: Canada
Type: Manipulative
Players: 2
Age: 7–10
Equipment: 1 hoop and 1 beanbag

►►HOW TO PLAY

One player holds a hoop so that it is vertical and resting on the ground. The other player stands three or four meters away and throws the beanbag over the hoop. If the beanbag goes over the hoop, she runs and jumps over the hoop. If it goes through the hoop, she runs and crawls through the hoop. And, if it lands anywhere else, she skips around the hoop and back to her starting position. Players change positions and repeat the game.

FIGURE 8.35   One player holds the hoop . . .

►►TIN CAN TOSS

Country: Mexico
Type: Ball and manipulative
Players: 5
Age: 8–10
Equipment: Cans and ball

FIGURE 8.36   Keep trying to hit the ball . . .

➤➤HOW TO PLAY

Five players form a circle and each player holds a tin can with one hand against the closed end and the other hand grasping the edges of the open end. On a signal, the ball is hit into the air to any other player. Players keep trying to hit the ball as many times as possible before it falls to the ground. When the ball touches the ground, the game starts over.

►►►Chapter Nine

NEW COOPERATIVE GAMES FOR SIX TO FIFTEEN PLAYERS

This chapter includes a selection of the special challenges made up by the teachers who participated in this project. They were asked to limit the number of players to no less than six and no more than fifteen. They could impose their own limitations with respect to equipment, skills, and rules. It was necessary, however, that their challenge include one or more elements of a cooperative game. The challenges that were created by the teachers produced a variety of interesting games. For example, "Bomb in the Box" from England resulted from the challenge, "Make up a game that has six players. You must use a hoop and a skipping rope. Your game must have equal turns, everyone must take part, and you must use trust in your game." The way the challenge was presented indicated that it was for children around eight years of age. The game that was produced met all the requirements of the challenge. The child's drawing (page 179) indicates how well he understood and enjoyed the game. It was interesting to note that most of the games involved manipulating a variety of small equipment, such as hoops, ropes, and stones. All the games met the requirement of at least two elements of a cooperative game.

►►FROG, JUMP, AND SLIDE

Country: South Africa
Type: Manipulative
Players: 5–6 per group
Age: 8–12
Equipment: None

Name of Game	Country	Type	Players	Age	Equipment	Page
Frog, Jump, and Slide	South Africa	Manipulative	5–6	8–12	None	177
Tallia	Greece	Manipulative	12	8–12	None	178
Bomb in the Box	England	Manipulative	6	8–12	Hoop, rope	179
Blind Flight	Luxembourg	Manipulative	10	10–12	Rope, cones	179
Copy Us	Jamaica	Manipulative	12	7–9	None	180
Captain's Ride	Argentina	Manipulative	7–8	10–12	Rope, tire	181
Interceptor	New Zealand	Ball	8	9–12	Ball	181
Crossover Blanket Volleyball	U.S.A.	Ball	12–14	10–12	Ball, net	182
Give and Take	Zimbabwe	Manipulative	10–15	8–12	Stones	182
Nine-Person Skip	Japan	Manipulative	6–9	8–12	Rope	183
Weird Wheel	Austria	Manipulative	6–15	9–12	None	183
Neckball Pass	Austria	Manipulative	6–15	7–9	Ball	183

▶▶HOW TO PLAY

Each group of five or six players begins by standing in a row, one behind the other with their legs apart. The last person starts crawling through the legs. As soon as she has passed two players, the next person begins and so on until the last child has crawled through the group. Next, the players spread apart but remain in a row and each child leapfrogs over every other member of the team. Finally,

FIGURE 9.1   ... last person starts crawling ...

the front player leads her team around a full circle and back to the starting position. Last player moves to the front of the line and repeats the game. The game continues until players are back in their original positions.

▶▶TALLIA

Country: Greece
Type: Manipulative
Players: 12
Age: 8–12
Equipment: None

▶▶HOW TO PLAY

Arrange the class into groups of twelve players. One half of each group forms a line and the first player holds on to a tree or another stable object. Each player then places his head

FIGURE 9.2   ... climbs on their backs ...

between the legs of the player directly in front of him. The remaining six players climb on their backs and stay there until the leader counts to a certain number. If all six players stay on for the full count, they score one point. If any player touches the ground during the counting, they start over. To repeat the game, the players reverse roles.

➤➤BOMB IN THE BOX

Country: England
Type: Manipulative
Players: 6
Age: 8–12
Equipment: 1 hoop and 1 skip rope

FIGURE 9.3   Number one places the hoop on . . .

➤➤HOW TO PLAY

Players line up as shown in the drawing. Number 1 places her hoop on her foot. Without using her hands, she passes it "footwise" to player number 2. Each player repeats this movement until the hoop reaches player Number 4. Player Number 4 must now lift the hoop over the rope without using her hands, and then exchange positions with player Number 6. Player Number 6 picks up the hoop with his foot, returns to the front of the line, and passes the hoop to player Number 2. The rotation continues until everyone has had a turn.

➤➤BLIND FLIGHT

Country: Luxembourg
Type: Manipulative
Players: 10
Age: 10–12
Equipment: 1 rope and 4 traffic cones

FIGURE 9.4   The guide tries to lead . . .

►►HOW TO PLAY

The first nine players hold the rope at the sides of their bodies, and place a paper bag over their heads. The last player (Guide) arranges the four traffic cones, comes back to his group, and teaches them three nonverbal commands. These are: (1) "Pull right" means the front player turns right; (2) "Pull left" means the front player turns left; (3) "Pull on both" means the front player moves straight ahead. The Guide then tries to lead the group to the first traffic cone. When the front player touches the first traffic cone, he places the cone in another spot and then exchanges positions with the Guide. The old Guide takes the paper bag and moves to the back of the group to become the last player. The group continues to the next cone, changes players, and continues this pattern to the last player.

►►COPY US

Country: Jamaica
Type: Manipulative
Players: 12
Age: 7–9
Equipment: None

FIGURE 9.5   . . . to demonstrate their original . . .

➤➤HOW TO PLAY

Children are allowed to choose their partners, and then everyone forms a circle. Each pair takes their turn to demonstrate their original movement. As new pairs come to the center, they cannot repeat the activity of any previous couple.

➤➤CAPTAIN'S RIDE

Country: Argentina
Type: Manipulative
Players: 7–8
Age: 10–12
Equipment: 2 long ropes and an old tire

➤➤HOW TO PLAY

Players tie two long ropes to an old tire. Three players hold on to each rope. The seventh player, the Captain, balances on the tire while the Crew of six drags the

FIGURE 9.6   The "Captain" balances on the tire . . .

tire seven to ten meters along the ground. Both the Crew and Captain attempt a good ride without the Captain falling off the tire. Each player rotates to the Captain's position.

➤➤INTERCEPTOR

Country: New Zealand
Type: Ball
Players: 8
Age: 9–12
Equipment: 1 soccer ball

FIGURE 9.7   Player number one starts . . .

➤➤HOW TO PLAY

Players one to seven scatter anywhere in the playing area. Player Number 1 starts dribbling the ball from one end of the field to the opposite end. He must pass the ball to each player as he moves toward the opposite end, turns around, and repeats the same action until he reaches player Number 2. Players 1 and 2 exchange positions and player 2 dribbles the ball to the starting line, then begins his turn. The game is repeated for every player.

➤➤CROSSOVER BLANKET VOLLEYBALL

Country: United States
Type: Ball
Players: 12–14
Age: 10–12
Equipment: 1 ball and net

➤➤HOW TO PLAY

Arrange two teams of six or seven players on each side of a volleyball net (a rope will do). Each team holds a blanket, keeping the net side open. One team starts with the ball on the blanket and tries to flip it over the net to the other team. As soon as the ball leaves the blanket, one player from the "sending team"

FIGURE 9.8   . . . and tries to flip it over . . .

crosses under the net and joins the other team. The receiving team tries to catch the ball in the blanket and return it to the other team. Each time the ball is returned, a player crosses under the net. One "collective" point is awarded to the group each time the ball crosses over the net and is successfully caught.

➤➤SUGGESTIONS AND VARIATIONS

1. Try the same game with two or three players crossing under the net after each toss.
2. Play the same game with different types and sizes of balls.
3. Play the same game with two or more balls (all the balls must be tossed together).

➤➤GIVE AND TAKE

Country: Zimbabwe
Type: Manipulative
Players: 10–15
Age: 8–12
Equipment: Stones

➤➤HOW TO PLAY

Ten players form a circle, kneel, and hold a stone in their right hand. On a signal from a player, all the players pass the stone along the ground and in front of the player on their right side. As the stone is

FIGURE 9.9   . . . all players pass the stone along . . .

passed, all the players call out "One." Passing and counting continues until the group calls out "Ten." The game is then repeated by passing the stones in the opposite direction.

▶▶NINE-PERSON SKIP

Country: Japan
Type: Manipulative
Players: 6–9
Age: 8–12
Equipment: Long rope

FIGURE 9.10   . . . and all the players jump the rope . . .

▶▶HOW TO PLAY

Six to nine players stand next to a rope. On a signal, outside players turn the rope and all players jump rope.

▶▶SUGGESTIONS AND VARIATIONS

1. Start the game with three or four players, and gradually increase the number.
2. Have each jumper enter separately.
3. Have the jumpers hold or bounce a ball.
4. Have the players touch the ground with their fingers after each jump.

▶▶WEIRD WHEEL

Country: Austria
Type: Manipulative
Players: 6–15
Age: 9–12
Equipment: None

FIGURE 9.11   . . . begins to rotate around . . .

▶▶HOW TO PLAY

The group joins hands and forms a circle. One player is chosen to be It and stands in the middle with arms stretched sideways and eyes closed. Circle players release their hands and move closer to the middle player, then stop and remain in this position for the remainder of the game. On a signal, It must stay in the same spot and begin to rotate her body around, changing the level of her arms by bending her knees or kneeling. It may also reverse directions at any time during the game. As It rotates her body, all the other players try to avoid being touched by It by bending down, stretching sideways, or backward, or jumping over Its arm if rotating in a low kneeling position. After a few minutes, the center player is changed and the game is repeated.

▶▶NECKBALL PASS

Country: Austria
Type: Manipulative

Players: 6–15
Age: 7–9
Equipment: 1 ball

►►HOW TO PLAY

Players scatter in the playing area and hold their hands behind their backs. One player places the ball under his chin and then puts his hands behind his back. The player with the ball tries to pass it to another player who has to receive it under her chin without using any other part of her body. If the ball is dropped, the player who tried to pass the ball picks it up, places it under her chin, and tries to pass it back to the same person. Once

FIGURE 9.12   . . . places it under her chin . . .

the group learns to pass the ball from neck to neck, try other positions, such as holding the ball between the elbows, knees, or even upside down with the legs up and the ball held between the feet.

►►►Chapter Ten

NEW COOPERATIVE GAMES FOR SIXTEEN OR MORE PLAYERS

The challenges in this chapter were some of the most difficult. As mentioned in Chapter 6, making up a game for a large number of players is a major task for young children. In the first eight games listed below the challenge was, "See if you can make up a game for the whole group, using all the available space, and no equipment. Your game must stress participation and equality." In this challenge, the complexity of the task is increased by requiring the players to use all available space and to play without any equipment. The additional requirement of including the elements of participation and equality added even more to the difficulty to the task. The games that resulted ranged from running and tag activities to group statues that represented geometrical shapes and animals that moved in a variety of ways and directions. The remaining six games were the result of special challenges made up by a few participating teachers. The challenges they presented included at least two of the six elements of a cooperative game. All of the games show that children interpret each challenge in their own unique way, and that each group draws on its inherent creative abilities in a collaborative way.

►►ZUMKHA

Country: India
Type: Run
Players: Class
Age: 7–10
Equipment: None

Name of Game	Country	Type	Players	Age	Equipment	Page
Zumkha	India	Run	16 or more	7–10	None	185
Robots	Germany	Manipulative	16 or more	8–12	None	186
Animals	New Zealand	Manipulative	16 or more	9–12	None	187
Humpy, Bumpy Caterpillar	Australia	Manipulative	16 or more	9–12	None	187
Grasshopper	Peru	Manipulative	16 or more	7–10	None	188
The Worm	Greece	Manipulative	16 or more	8–12	None	188
Sculptor	Austria	Manipulative	16 or more	9–12	None	189
Continuous Motion	Czech Republic	Run	16 or more	7–10	None	189
Pirates	Germany	Ball	16 or more	8–12	Hoops	190
Mat Pull	Japan	Manipulative	16 or more	8–12	Mats	191
Bildaren	Sweden	Tag	16 or more	9–12	Mat	191
Robot Game	Austria	Manipulative	16 or more	7–10	Pencils	192
Moving Musical Hoops	Canada	Manipulative	16 or more	8–12	Hoops	193
Geometry Class	Argentina	Manipulative	16 or more	8–12	Paper	193

➤➤HOW TO PLAY

The class begins in a large circle facing counterclockwise. The teacher stands in the middle and signals the class to walk, run, or perform any other type of locomotor movement. As the players are moving, the teacher calls out a number, such as "Five," signaling all the players to get into groups of five. Those players who fail to get into groups according to the called number must say a rhyme or perform a trick before the game begins again. The game always starts with all players in a circle formation.

➤➤ROBOTS

Country: Germany
Type: Manipulative
Players: 3 per group
Age: 8–12
Equipment: None

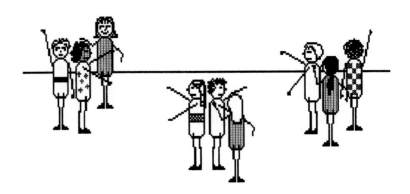

FIGURE 10.1   . . . by slightly touching them . . .

➤➤HOW TO PLAY

Arrange the class into groups of three. Two players are the Robots, and the other player is the Engineer who steers the robots. The Robots can only move forward and make right-angle turns. To start, the Robots stand back-to-back, and the engineer begins to move the robots by slightly touching them on their right shoulders (right-angle turn), left shoulders (left-angle turn), or head (straight ahead one step). The task of the Engineer is to move the Robots so they face each other, stand side by side, or face one behind the other. Players change positions after the Robots are facing whatever position they agreed on. The next game can be played with the Robots keeping their eyes closed.

➤➤ANIMALS

Country: New Zealand
Type: Manipulative
Players: Class
Age: 9–12
Equipment: None

➤➤HOW TO PLAY

Divide the class into two or three groups of ten to twelve players in each

FIGURE 10.2   . . . has two heads, twelve legs . . .

group. The teacher describes an imaginary animal. The imaginary animal might be something like, "It has two heads, twelve legs, and one tail." Each group then decides how they will create and illustrate this animal. One additional rule is added—the animal must move ten yards.

➤➤HUMPY, BUMPY CATERPILLAR

Country: Australia
Type: Manipulative
Players: Class
Age: 9–12
Equipment: None

FIGURE 10.3   . . . longest walking caterpillar . . .

➤➤HOW TO PLAY

The whole class attempts to make the longest walking caterpillar by joining together as follows: 1. One child crouches on her hands and knees; 2. the second child stretches over the top of the first child so that her hands and feet are in contact with the floor; 3. the third child holds on to the first child's ankles while her own knees touch the floor; 4. the fourth child assumes the same position as number two; 5. once the class has assembled the caterpillar, they try to move forward without breaking apart.

▶▶GRASSHOPPER

Country: Peru
Type: Manipulative
Players: Class
Age: 7–10
Equipment: Small object

FIGURE 10.4   . . . the "Grasshopper" stands inside . . .

▶▶HOW TO PLAY

Arrange the players in pairs and form a large circle with partners standing side by side. One pair is chosen to be the Grasshopper and they stand inside the circle, back-to-back, elbows locked, and balance a small object between their shoulders. They must stay about one meter away from the circle players. As the circle players begin to clap their hands, the two inside players must start jumping clockwise around the circle, keeping their elbows locked, balancing the object between their shoulders, and keeping time to the rhythm of the children's clapping. Circle players may speed up or slow down the speed of their clapping. If the Grasshopper drops the object, they change places with the couple closest to them and the game begins again. If the Grasshopper makes it around the circle without dropping the object, they change places with the next pair.

▶▶THE WORM

Country: Greece
Type: Manipulative
Players: 16 or more
Age: 8–12
Equipment: None

▶▶HOW TO PLAY

One child is selected to be the leader. All the remaining players line up behind the leader and place their hands on the knees of the player immediately in front of them. When everyone is ready, the leader begins to move forward and then starts to move in various directions. Everyone tries to keep in contact until the teacher signals them to stop. The last player in the line becomes the new leader and the movement is repeated.

▶▶SUGGESTIONS AND VARIATIONS

1. The players change the position of their hands, such as holding hands on their shoulders, head, or ankles.
2. The last player in line becomes the leader and everyone moves backward.

FIGURE 10.5   . . . the leader begins to move . . .

➤➤SCULPTOR

Country: Austria
Type: Manipulative
Players: 16 or more
Age: 9–12
Equipment: None

➤➤HOW TO PLAY

One player is selected to be the Sculptor and stands in front of the group. The Sculptor chooses the first player to make the first unusual and funny position. This player remains in this position throughout the game. As each player is selected, he must be in contact with the previously chosen

FIGURE 10.6   . . . he/she must keep in contact with . . .

player. When the last player is part of the sculpture, the Sculptor then becomes the last part of the sculpture.

➤➤CONTINUOUS MOTION

Country: Czech Republic
Type: Run
Players: 16 or more
Age: 7–10
Equipment: None

➤➤HOW TO PLAY

Designate a number of spots in the playing area (use hoops, sticks, etc.) to represent every player in the group. Players are numbered and line up behind the starting line. On a signal, player Number 1 runs to the first spot and balances on one foot. The second player runs to player Number 1, touches him, and assumes his position and stance. Player Number 1 runs to the next spot and resumes balancing on one foot. The third player, and so on, continues the process until the last player is on spot Number 1.

➤➤SUGGESTIONS AND VARIATIONS

1. Repeat the game by changing the action to jumping on the spot or balancing on other parts of the body.
2. Repeat the game by changing the method of moving from spot to spot, such as skipping, moving on all fours, or moving like different types of animals.

➤➤PIRATES

Country: Germany
Type: Ball
Players: Class
Age: 8–12
Equipment: 15–20 hoops and 6–8 balls

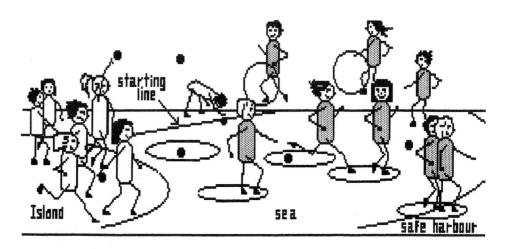

FIGURE 10.7   One half of the group are "Pirates" . . .

➤➤HOW TO PLAY

The playing area is divided into an Island, a Safe Harbor, and the Sea, as shown in the illustration. One half of the class are Pirates and must stay in the Island area. The other half are Traders and must move their Ships (hoops) from the starting line across the Sea, by only using their feet, to the Safe Harbor. If a Pirate throws the ball and hits the hoop or lands inside it, the Ship sinks. However, the Trader inside a sinking Ship may jump to the nearest Ship and help move it to the Safe Harbor. The sinking Trader is allowed only one jump to reach the other Ship, and may have to wait for another Trader to move close to him. When this Ship reaches the Safe Harbor, the pair separates and the Trader who was sunk returns to his

Ship and continues his voyage. The other Trader must pick up his Ship and walk back to the starting line around the outside of the playing area and begin again. If a Pirate throws a ball that does not hit a Ship, he waits until it has stopped moving and then touches another Pirate who is to go and retrieve the ball. When the retrieving Pirate picks up a ball, he must move outside the playing area and run back to his Island before he takes his turn to throw the ball. The game ends after a time limit or if all the Ships are sunk at the same time and there are no seaworthy Ships to rescue the sinking Traders.

►►MAT PULL

Country: Japan
Type: Manipulative
Players: 16 or more
Age: 8–12
Equipment: Mats

FIGURE 10.8   . . . to pull as many players off . . .

►►HOW TO PLAY

Divide the class into two equal teams. Team A stands on the mat and team B stands around the mat. The object of the game is for the players on team B to pull as many team A players as they can off the mat. Players on the mat may help each other by holding teammates; however, hitting, striking, or any other harmful movements are not permitted. Once a player is pulled off the mat, she must stay clear of the mat until the game is completed. After a set time limit, the teams exchange positions. The team with the largest number remaining on the mat wins the game.

►►BILDAREN

Country: Sweden
Type: Tag
Players: Class
Age: 9–12
Equipment: 1 large mat

►►HOW TO PLAY

One large mat (hospital) is placed in the center of the floor. One player is selected to be the Bildaren, who tries to tag other players. If a player is tagged (Car Accident),

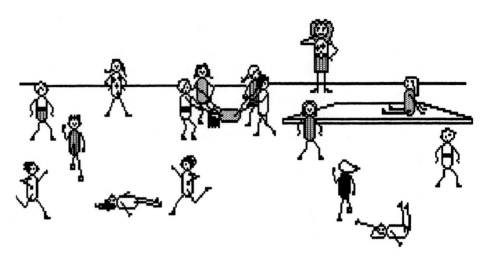

FIGURE 10.9   . . . and may carry the injured player . . .

he must lie down on the floor and become an Injured Person. Any four players may run to the hospital mat, and if not tagged before they reach it, they are safe. They are then Immune and may carry the injured player back to the Hospital mat where he is then free to join the game again and the Rescuers are no longer Immune. When the Bildaren has four Injured players on the floor, he changes places with the first person tagged.

►►ROBOT GAME

Country: Austria
Type: Manipulative
Players: 16 or more
Age: 7–10
Equipment: Pencils or small objects

►►HOW TO PLAY

The game can be played in the classroom or outdoors within a designated playing area. The obstacles in the classroom would be desks, tables, wastepaper baskets, and so on. Place the hoops, traffic cones, or boxes in the outdoor playing area. Four players are chosen to be the Humans and each holds a pencil in one hand. All the other players are Robots and must keep their eyes closed and move in a slow, robotlike fashion. Robots also have additional limitations: They cannot hear or speak. On a signal, everyone begins to move through the playing area. When a Robot brushes against a Human, the Human drops her pencil and immediately turns into a Robot. Also, when a Robot touches an obstacle, it must remain still and wait to be saved by a Human. If a Human can guide two Robots so they touch each other, both Robots turn into Humans. The game continues for a designated period of time or until all the players have been turned into Robots.

FIGURE 10.10 **"Ten"**

➤➤MOVING MUSICAL HOOPS

Country: Canada
Type: Manipulative
Players: Class
Age: 8–12
Equipment: 1 set of hoops

➤➤HOW TO PLAY

Every player starts inside his hoop and begins to run anywhere within the playing area. As the players are running, the teacher calls out "Two" and all players must link up in twos and keep running. The game continues with the teacher calling out "Three," "Four," and so forth, until the whole class is entangled in the hoops and all are running in the same direction together.

➤➤SUGGESTION AND VARIATION

Place the hoops on the floor and gradually remove one or more hoops as children are running through the area. When you call "Stop," players must stand inside a hoop. Gradually remove all but one or two hoops and require everyone to stay inside their hoops. The latter situation is fun for everyone—including the instructor!

➤➤Geometry Class

Country: Argentina
Type: Manipulative
Players: Class
Age: 8–12
Equipment: None

FIGURE 10.11   Team "A" forms the geometrical shape . . .

➤➤HOW TO PLAY

The class is divided into two teams. Each team writes the name of five different geometrical shapes on separate pieces of paper, then places them face down in the middle of the playing area. One player from team A selects one of the ten pieces of paper, reads the name of the shape to himself, then whispers it to his teammates. Team A forms the geometrical shape then team B tries to guess its name. Teams exchange positions after each shape is formed and the winner is the team that correctly guesses the highest number of geometrical shapes.

Chapter Eleven

HOW TO HELP CHILDREN INVENT THEIR OWN COOPERATIVE GAMES

Webster's Dictionary defines *cooperation* as "the association of persons for common benefit." On the basis of this definition, any competitive game, such as volleyball, basketball, or dodgeball, would meet this criterion, because a measure of cooperation is required if a team is to win a contest. The contemporary meaning of *cooperative games,* however, goes beyond *Webster's* definition. The cooperative games described in Chapters 8, 9, and 10 are essentially noncompetitive activities that emphasize the interaction of people rather than the game or the final score. They normally stress the elements of fun, cooperation, equality, participation, success, and trust. Each of these distinguishing characteristics or elements of cooperative behavior are described below. Following this, the game of Crossover Blanket Volleyball (page 182) is used to illustrate how and where each element is emphasized in the rules and the way the game is played. Other games, such as Hoopscotch (page 162), Modified Musical Chairs (page 198), and Juggle a Number (page 176), could serve the same function. The latter part of this chapter describes and illustrates how to present a series of cooperative game challenges in a systematic and sequential way.

➤➤FUN

Everyone must receive a measure of enjoyment from playing the game. The game encourages the players to laugh with, not at, others as they play. And, when finished playing, all players leave the "magic circle" of play with a sense of joy and happiness.

Volleyball has been a favorite game of young children for many years, but it is a competitive activity with winners and losers. Crossover Blanket Volleyball, with players constantly changing sides, and total group scoring rather than individual team scoring, eliminates the pressure of winning. The new rules encourage children to play because the game is not only fun and exciting to play, but its structure also encourages positive social interaction among all players.

FIGURE 11.1   Crossover Blanket Volleyball

▶▶COOPERATION

Everyone must work together to achieve a common goal. Cooperation involves helping each other and sharing each task as the group moves toward its common goal. In Crossover Blanket Volleyball, every player must cooperate or the ball can not be caught or propelled over the net. In addition, the new rotation system ensures that every player has a chance to share each task and to learn to help in different group efforts as he or she crosses under the net to join a new group.

▶▶EQUALITY

Everyone has an equal role in the game; that is, each player "hits the ball" roughly the same number of times as any other player, "rotates" to every other position, and, in part of the game, assumes the leadership role on a rotational basis. The rules of this modified version of volleyball require every player to rotate his or her position on the blanket as well as from one blanket to the other. This ensures the equality of all players throughout the game.

▶▶PARTICIPATION

Everyone is actively involved in the game. The rules of the game cannot eliminate any player from playing. If a player is "hit," "touched," or misses a "hit" or "catch," she continues to play. Requiring a team effort every time the ball is flipped or caught ensures that everyone has an active and continuous role to play throughout the game. Rotation of players to the opposite side guarantees additional movement on the part of all players. This rule also stresses participating in a total group effort rather than on separate teams.

▶▶SUCCESS

Everyone experiences a sense of accomplishment. Cooperative games have no losers. Success must be personally defined rather than determined by a score or group standard. Because the score is kept for the whole group, there are no losers in this game. Also, the act of flipping or catching is also a measure of how well the group cooperatively performs. The individual's measure of success centers on how the individual player felt about her contribution as she helped perform each of the collective movements.

▶▶TRUST

Everyone must be able to place a measure of trust in other players. This means that situations within the game require a player to rely on another player to "miss him," "hold him," "balance him," or perform a movement that considers his safety and well-being. There is a slight measure of trust in this game. It is the part of the game that requires all players to hold the blanket and execute the required movement in unison. This is, by comparison to all others, a relatively weak game to illustrate the element of trust. However, the reader will be able to find games in Chapters 8, 9, and 10 where trust is clearly illustrated.

These six elements of a cooperative game were selected on the basis of a review of articles and books dealing with cooperative games, plus information obtained from field studies of young children. During the past several years, teachers and recreation instructors from many countries have suggested that other elements, such as "sharing" and "fairness" or "sportsmanship," be added to the list. It is suggested that the list be modified or expanded by each instructor to meet the needs of their own social and geographical conditions.

The process used in guiding children to create their own cooperative games is an extension of the approach used when teaching creative games. To illustrate, the first four columns in the accompanying chart are used to set limitations for children to create their own games. If we pose a challenge, such as "Make up a game with your partner, in your own space, using one ball and two hoops and a dribble," children may or may not create a cooperative game. Their game might become a dribbling contest around the hoops or a cooperative game, such as dribbling and passing as each player dribbles around his own hoop. By adding the fifth column, Cooperative Elements, to the accompanying table we can guide children to develop a new creative game that also emphasizes one or more of the elements of fun, cooperation, equality, participation, success, and trust.

Creative Games Chart

Number of Players	Playing Space	Equipment	Skills and Rules	Cooperative Elements
From individual activities	From limited space	From use of simple equipment	From single skills and rules	Fun, Cooperation, Equality, Participation, Trust, and Success
To	To	To	To	
Partner activities	Use of more space	Use of more varied and complex equipment	Use of more complex skills and rules	
To				
Group activities				

There is one general comment made by numerous teachers and recreation instructors who have used the cooperative games approach. They have consistently found that, if children do not understand the meaning of these elements there is, in almost every instance, little chance of a cooperative game being produced. For this reason, teach the children the meaning of the cooperative elements before posing any challenges involving these words. This can be accomplished by teaching them the following cooperative games in order to illustrate and discuss each element in a practical and understandable way.

▶▶GAME 1: STICK EXCHANGE (see page 160)

Arrange your group in partners and have them play **Stick Exchange.** This is a good example of the element, **Equality,** because each player has an equal role to play throughout the game. It also demonstrates the need for players to **Trust** each other during each maneuver of the game. After a few minutes, have everyone find a new partner and repeat the game. After a few more minutes, stop the game and have everyone come together in one large group. Ask the group what they thought of this game: Was it fun, difficult, and so on. As the discussion proceeds, explain how each player had an equal role and how there was a need to trust each other throughout the game. Arrange the group into new sets of partners and play one or two other cooperative games involving two players, such as Under Ball (page 158) Double Tug (page 160), and Blind Horse (page 163). Follow up each game with a discussion about the elements of equality and trust. When you think the children understand and can describe the meaning of *equality* and *trust,* move on to the next game.

▶▶GAME 2: JUGGLE A NUMBER (see page 176)

This game is played with five or six players and emphasizes several cooperative elements. The first element, **Cooperation,** is one of the most important because each player must be aware of where the other players are, who to pass to, and when. Without this cooperation, the game ends in chaos. Every player plays the same role as any other player so the element of **Equality** is also represented. And, when everyone cooperates and passes the ball at the strategic time, each player as well as the group, reaps a measure of **Success.** After playing a few games, stop the game and explain to the group the meaning and importance of cooperation. Point out that everyone must be striving toward a common goal and how each player's contribution was equal to everyone else's. The last point, **Success,** is measured in two ways. First, when each player knows she has passed the ball at the correct moment and to the right player, there is an immediate feeling of personal success and accomplishment. When a group of five players can keep all five balls constantly in the air for a reasonable length of time, there is excitement as well as a group feeling of success through a genuine team effort. In discussions with children, these points will normally be expressed by the players in their own way but reflecting a similar point of view. Now move on to a game involving the whole group.

▶▶GAME 3: MODIFIED MUSICAL CHAIRS (see page 199)

Musical Chairs is an excellent game to begin with, and then it can be followed by the modified version. This game starts with six to eight chairs lined up back-to-back in the middle of the playing area. All the players scatter around the chairs; then the music begins and everyone must move clockwise around the chairs. When the music stops, everyone tries to sit in the chairs. Players who are sitting in a chair stay in the game, and all other players are eliminated and must stay away from the chairs. One or two chairs are removed and the game is repeated. The

FIGURE 11.2   The game continues until . . .

game continues until the last player is sitting on the remaining chair. This form of Musical Chairs is fun at the very beginning, but the quick elimination of so many players and the notion of just one winner and everyone else as losers is clearly illustrated in this game.

Modified Musical Chairs begins in the same way as the original game, but that's about all. In this new version, when the music stops, everyone tries to sit in the chairs. However, in this case, as soon as the chairs are full, remaining players may sit on the knees of any sitting player. It is quite possible that one sitting player may not have anyone sitting on his knees, while another

FIGURE 11.3   . . . may sit on the knees . . .

player may have six to eight players in a line in front of him. The music begins again and everyone starts to move around the chairs. As the players are moving, the instructor removes one or two chairs. The game continues until one chair remains with one long line of sitting players.

All the elements of a cooperative game are represented in Modified Musical Chairs. When children discuss this game, they usually say this version is a lot more fun. This is an opportune time for the instructor to review the six elements to make sure the children not only understand their meaning but can also can verbally explain each in a clear and concise manner.

When you feel that the children understand the meaning and importance of these terms, pose a cooperative game challenge that stresses one or more of the elements listed in the last column of the Creative Games Chart (page 197). Although each game usually stresses all six cooperative elements, the important aspect of each challenge is to get children to think consciously about one or two and stress them in their own game. The following examples will give the reader an idea of how to present a series of challenges.

➤➤CHALLENGES INVOLVING TWO PLAYERS AND STRESSING COOPERATION AND TRUST

The first sentence in the following challenge allows the two players maximum freedom to select the number and type of small equipment they want to use in their game. The two cooperative elements of **Cooperation** and **Trust,** specified in the second sentence, ensure that these two elements will be present in their game.

> **Challenge:** "See if you can invent a game with your partner using one or more pieces of small equipment. Your game must stress cooperation and must, in some way, place trust in the other player."

A challenge similar to the one above was presented to children in various countries around the world. The following list of games they developed also stressed cooperation and trust as well as equality and participation.

1. Under Ball (Botswana, page 158)
2. Jump Hoop (England, page 158)
3. Double Tug (South Africa, page 160)
4. Hoopscotch (Canada, page 162)

➤➤CHALLENGES INVOLVING THREE PLAYERS AND STRESSING PARTICIPATION AND SUCCESS

The first part of the following challenge has two main restrictions. These are: the children can only use one ball in their game and are limited to two pieces of small equipment. However, if available, they may be able to choose from a wide selection of small equipment. The second part of the challenge requires that each player demonstrate an element of cooperation in whatever game they eventually create. Cooperation between two players is fairly easy; with three players, there is a need for more ongoing discussion in the planning phase as well as in the eventual execution of the game. The requirement to include an element of success meant care had to be taken to design a game that was easy enough for each player to perform in order to immediately experience a sense of success.

> **Challenge:** See if your group of three can make up a game with one ball, one goal, and dribble the ball with your feet. Your game must stress participation and success.

The games listed below are examples of the kind of games children will create from a similar type of challenge:

1. Circle Goal (Jamaica, page 167)
2. Snabbmal (Sweden, page 168)
3. Soccer Circuit (New Zealand, page 171)

➤➤CHALLENGES INVOLVING THE WHOLE GROUP AND STRESSING PARTICIPATION AND EQUALITY

Making up a game for the whole group is a major task for young children. In addition, the complexity of the task is increased by requiring the players to use all available space and to play without any equipment. The requirement of including the elements of participation and equality add even more to the complexity of the task and makes this a real challenge for the children.

> **Challenge:** See if you can make up a game for the whole class, using all the available space, and no equipment. Your game must stress *participation* and *equality*.

The games that resulted from presenting this challenge to children from a variety of cultural and geographical backgrounds are listed below.

1. Geometry Class (Argentina, page 193)
2. Bildaren (Sweden, page 191)
3. Sculptor (Austria, page 189)

It is strongly recommended that when you begin to pose the first few cooperative game challenges, you start with just two players, require a minimum of skills and rules, and stress one or two elements of a cooperative game. Gradually increase the number of players and add more skills and rules and cooperative elements as the children demonstrate their ability to handle more complex challenges.

One final comment: When children are given the opportunity and accompanying freedom, they will invent very imaginative and enjoyable games. Keep a notepad handy and record the games you think should be saved so other children will be able to play them. Like the games contained in Parts Two and Three, they will become part of an expanded games resource file for all children to enjoy.

➤➤➤

BIBLIOGRAPHY

Alliance for Health, Physical Education, Recreation and Dance. (1976). *ICPHER Book of Worldwide Games and Dances.* Reston, VA: AAHPER.

Avedon, E. M. and Sutton-Smith, B. (1971). *The Study of Games.* New York: John Wiley and Sons.

Barbarash, L. (1997). *Multicultural Games.* Champaign, IL: Human Kinetics.

Bett, H. (1968). *The Games of Children: Their Origin and History.* Detroit, MI: Singing Tree Press.

Botermans, J. (1989). *The World of Games: Their Origin and History, How to Play Them, and How to Make Them.* New York: Facts on File.

Fluegelman, A. (1981). *More New Games.* New York: Doubleday.

Fowke, E. (1988). *Red Rover Red Rover, Children's Games Played in Canada.* Toronto, ON: Doubleday.

Grunfeld, F., Ed. (1975). *Games of the World.* New York: Holt, Rinehart and Winston.

Kirchner, G. and Fishburne, G. (1997). *Physical Education for Elementary School Children,* 10th Ed. Dubuque, IA: McGraw-Hill Co.

Lucas, E. V. and Lucas, E. (1900). *Three Hundred Games and Pastimes,* 3rd Ed. Edinburgh, Scotland: R. Clark.

Milberg, A. (1976). *Street Games.* New York: McGraw-Hill Co.

Mohr, M. S. (1993). *The Games Treasury.* Shelburne, VT: Chapters Publishing.

Opie, I. P. (1984). *Children's Games in Streets and Playgrounds.* New York: Oxford University Press.

Orlick, T. (1978). *The Cooperative Games and Sports Book.* New York: Pantheon Books.

Sierra, J. and Kaminski, R. (1995). *Children's Traditional Games.* Phoenix, AR: Oryx Press.

Strutt, J. (1898). *Sports and Pastimes of the People of England.* London: Chatto and Windus.

Sutton-Smith, B. (1976). *A Children's Games Anthology: Studies in Folklore and Anthropology.* New York: Aron Press.

Weinstein, M. and Goodman, J. (1980). *Playfair.* San Luis Obispo, CA: Impact Publishing.

GAMES BY COUNTRY

Name of Game	Type	Players	Age	Equipment	Page
ARGENTINA					
Headband Tag	Tag	16 or more	8–10	Headbands	134
Stolen Ball	Ball	16 or more	10–12	Ball	142
Polo	Manipulative	2	9–12	Ball, cones	161
Blind Horseman	Ball	3	8–12	Ball, stick	170
Captain's Ride	Manipulative	7–8	10–12	Rope, tire	181
Geometry Class	Manipulative	16 or more	8–12	Paper	193
AUSTRALIA					
Snow White	Run and Tag	16 or more	7–12	Hoops	8
Kickball	Ball	3	9–12	Ball	45
Hoop Tag	Ball	6	8–12	Ball, hoops	47
Super-Duper Hoop	Ball	2	8–12	Ball, hoops	88
Back-Pass Beanbag	Manipulative	5	9–12	Beanbags	98
Charge	Tag	16 or more	9–12	Sticks	132
Change the Spot	Tag	16 or more	8–12	None	144
Leap Ball	Ball	2	10–12	Ball, hoop	162
Hoop Soccer	Ball	3	9–12	Ball, basket	169
Seesaw	Manipulative	3	10–12	None	172
Humpy, Bumpy Caterpillar	Manipulative	16 or more	9–12	None	187
AUSTRIA					
Blind Snake	Manipulative	3 or more	7–10	Blindfolds	76
Blind Hen	Ball	10–14	9–12	Ball, shoes	115
Halli Hallo	Ball	7–8	7–12	Ball, hoop	120
Detective	Guessing	16 or more	9–12	None	127
Shoelace Catch	Manipulative	16 or more	9–12	Shoelaces	132
Weird Wheel	Manipulative	6–15	9–12	None	183
Neckball Pass	Manipulative	6–15	7–9	Ball	183
Sculptor	Manipulative	16 or more	9–11	None	189
Robot Game	Manipulative	16 or more	7–10	Pencils	192
BAHRAIN					
Loabat A-Haloo	Ball and Tag	5–7	8–12	Ball	28
BARBADOS					
Dog and Bone	Run and Tag	10–20	7–12	Stick	10
Cat and Rat	Run and Tag	16 or more	7–12	None	14
Through the Obstacle	Manipulative	5	7–12	Ball, chair	99
Four Squares	Ball	16 or more	10–12	Ball	138

(continued)

Name of Game	Type	Players	Age	Equipment	Page
BELGIUM					
Lemon, Lemon	Run	16 or more	8–12	Ball	20
Five-and-Ten Ball	Run and Tag	10–16	9–12	Bag	27
Telegram	Guessing	6–15	7–12	None	57
Klinkslagen	Manipulative	2	10–12	Sticks	64
Skittleball	Ball	2	10–12	Ball, cones	91
Foot Searching	Manipulative	2	9–12	Beanbag	101
Blindball	Ball	2	9–12	Ball	163
BOTSWANA					
Step on My Shadow	Run and Tag	16 or more	8–10	None	23
Kitchen Ball	Ball	16 or more	7–10	Ball	43
We Are from Tlhahana	Manipulative	16 or more	8–10	None	58
Bucket Ball	Ball	2	8–12	Ball, basket	88
Hidden Object	Manipulative	5	8–10	Small object	96
Three Sticks	Tag	16 or more	8–10	Ball	128
Piggyback Polo	Manipulative	16 or more	9–12	Ball	141
Underball	Ball	2	8–10	Ball	158
Three Boys	Ball	3	8–12	Ball	166
Jump Ball	Ball	3	8–10	Ball	173
BRAZIL					
Number Relay	Run	16 or more	9–12	Beanbag	27
Tampa	Manipulative	4	10–12	Caps	77
Jogo	Ball	4	9–12	Bats, cans	104
CANADA					
Kick the Can	Run and Tag	16 or more	8–12	Tin can	6
Emergency	Run and Tag	16 or more	8–12	None	22
Borden Ball	Ball	16 or more	9–12	Ball	38
Beanbag Pass	Ball	2	6–8	Beanbags	54
Catch a Falling Star	Ball	2	8–12	Ball, box	90
Two-Person Catch	Ball	2	7–10	Ball	93
Pattywhack	Manipulative	5	8–12	Beanbag	102
Scoops	Ball	6–14	7–10	Scoops, balls	117
Stick Tag	Tag	16 or more	7–10	Sticks and ribbons	135
Empire Strikes Back	Manipulative	16 or more	8–12	Balls	143
Hoopscotch	Manipulative	2	8–12	Hoops	162
Changing Positions	Manipulative	2	7–9	Hoops, bench	165
Firefighter Rescue	Ball	3	7–9	Ball, basket	170
Jumping the Hoop	Manipulative	2	7–10	Hoop, beanbag	175
Moving Musical Hoops	Manipulative	16 or more	8–12	Hoops	193
CHINA					
Drop the Hanky	Run	16 or more	6–9	Cloth	18
Electric Gate	Run and Tag	16 or more	9–12	None	26
Three Pin Tag	Tag	16 or more	9–12	Cones	129
Chase Me	Tag	16 or more	8–12	None	143
Under the Leg	Ball	3	8–12	Ball	166
CUBA					
La Tabla de Maní Picao	Manipulative	16 or more	7–10	Stones	74
Name the Animal	Ball	4	7–10	Balls, cards	109
Color Tag	Tag	16 or more	9–12	None	140

Name of Game	Type	Players	Age	Equipment	Page
CZECH REPUBLIC					
Shoot the Duck	Ball	10–16	8–12	Ball, box	49
Double the Fun	Ball	4	7–12	Balls	106
Fastest and Mostest	Ball	3–9	7–9	Ball	117
Friendly Knockout	Ball	16 or more	8–12	Ball	129
Gates	Tag	16 or more	8–12	None	146
Continuous Motion	Run	16 or more	7–10	None	189
DENMARK					
Open the Window	Run and Tag	7	9–12	None	29
Pinball	Ball	2	8–12	Ball, cones	105
ENGLAND					
Stuck in the Mud	Run and Tag	16 or more	7–12	None	12
Prisoner's Base	Run and Tag	16 or more	8–12	None	21
Beat the Ball	Ball	6–12	7–12	Ball	44
Queenie I.O.	Manipulative	5–7	6–9	Small object	59
Rock, Scissors, Paper	Manipulative	16 or more	9–12	None	70
North, East, South, West	Manipulative	16 or more	7–9	None	73
Butterflies	Ball	2	7–9	Ball, box	87
Ball in the Basket	Ball	2	6–8	Ball, basket	93
Catch a Caterpillar	Manipulative	5	9–12	Hoop, beanbag	95
Gold	Ball	6–15	7–12	Beanbag	110
Beats Me	Manipulative	10	8–12	Ball, hoop	114
Tag Bag	Tag	16 or more	7–12	Beanbag	126
Cold Winds	Tag	16 or more	7–10	Ribbons	137
Jump Hoop	Manipulative	2	7–10	Rope, hoop	158
Wall Catch	Ball	2	7–12	Ball	165
ABC Dribble	Ball	3	9–12	Ball, cones	169
Bomb in the Box	Manipulative	2	8–12	Hoop, rope	179
ESTONIA					
Chick Chickabiddy	Run and Tag	6–8	9–12	None	29
FRANCE					
Mic Mac Relay	Run	16 or more	9–12	None	24
The Fly	Ball	5–6	8–12	Ball	43
Flying Goalie	Ball	2	9–12	Ball, goal	90
Ball Thrower	Ball	2	9–12	Bat, ball	161
GERMANY					
Black Cat	Run and Tag	16 or more	8–10	Ropes	8
Brunt	Ball	12–20	9–12	Ball, cones	38
Gummi Twist	Manipulative	3–4	8–12	Elastic bands	55
Spacehopper Flight	Manipulative	2	8–10	Ball, darts	94
Merry-Go-Round	Manipulative	5	8–12	Ropes, beanbag	103
Hunter and Wolf	Tag	16 or more	8–10	Hoops, sticks	125
Fingertips	Manipulative	2	8–12	Small equipment	159
Blind Horse	Manipulative	2	10–12	Ropes	163
Robots	Manipulative	16 or more	8–12	None	186
Pirates	Ball	16 or more	8–12	Hoops	190

(continued)

Name of Game	Type	Players	Age	Equipment	Page
GHANA					
Sugar and Honey	Run	16 or more	6–9	None	31
GREECE					
Somersault	Run	16 or more	9–12	Rope	14
Carriage and Driver	Run and Tag	16 or more	9–12	None	30
Balls and Funnels	Ball	4	9–12	Ball, paper	51
Marbles	Manipulative	2–4	8–12	Marbles	60
Nose to Nose	Manipulative	6–15	7–9	Matchbox	121
The Statue	Manipulative	16 or more	7–10	None	125
Pair Tag	Tag	16 or more	7–12	None	140
Backside Throw	Ball	5	7–9	Ball	174
Tallia	Manipulative	12	8–12	None	178
The Worm	Manipulative	16 or more	8–12	None	188
HONG KONG					
Crosscut Beancurd	Run and Tag	5	7–9	None	32
HUNGARY					
Grab the Rag	Tag	5–10	9–12	Sticks, rag	121
INDIA					
KHO	Run and Tag	16 or more	8–12	None	26
Nirali Batel	Ball and Tag	16 or more	9–12	Ball	45
Tripple Dribble	Ball	3	9–12	Ball, cones	172
IRAN					
Omlar	Run and Tag	16 or more	9–12	None	31
Anou	Run	16 or more	10–12	None	137
ISRAEL					
Circle Balance	Ball	4	6–8	Ball, hoop	52
Country and City	Manipulative	2–3	7–10	Cards	75
Shooball	Manipulative	2	6–7	Ball, cones	105
Shoot the Top	Ball	5	7–9	Ball, hoops	108
Passing in the Square	Ball	4	7–9	Balls, balloons	173
ITALY					
Crab Soccer	Ball	16 or more	8–12	Ball	42
Palo Berni	Manipulative	5	9–12	Balloons, hoops	98
Scout Ball	Ball	16 or more	10–16	Ball, ribbons	133
Claudia Berni	Ball	3	9–12	Ball, cones	168
JAMAICA					
Circle Goal	Ball	3	9–12	Ball	167
Copy Us	Manipulative	12	7–9	None	180
JAPAN					
Alley Cat	Run and Tag	16 or more	8–12	None	23
Rocky Boat	Manipulative	7–8	10–12	None	58
Bubble	Manipulative	8–10	6–8	None	77
Hit the Ball	Ball	2	9–12	Ball, marbles	87

Name of Game	Type	Players	Age	Equipment	Page
JAPAN (cont.)					
Quick Number	Ball	5	8–12	Beanbag	97
Surround Tag	Tag	16 or more	8–12	Sticks	134
One, Two, Three Tag	Tag	16 or more	8–12	None	141
Stick Exchange	Manipulative	2	8–12	Sticks	160
Nine-Person Skip	Manipulative	6–9	8–12	Rope	183
Mat Pull	Manipulative	16 or more	8–12	Mats	191
KOREA					
Eyeglasses	Run and Tag	16 or more	7–10	None	28
LUXEMBOURG					
Divisible Snakes	Run and Tag	16 or more	8–12	None	24
Giischt	Manipulative	2–4	8–12	Sticks	65
Reaction Ball	Ball	2	8–12	Balls, cones	94
Twelve Big Eggs	Manipulative	5	9–12	Ball	97
Fir Cone Hide	Manipulative	5	8–12	Cones	102
One, Two, Three Catch	Tag	5–6	9–12	None	114
Blind Flight	Manipulative	10	10–12	Rope, cones	179
MEXICO					
Snake Bridges to Sea	Tag	5	7–9	None	32
Run Away Kitten	Ball	2–6	7–12	Ball	50
Beanbag Polo	Manipulative	4	9–12	Beanbag	108
El Bosque Encantado	Tag	10–15	7–9	None	118
Gallo Desplumado	Manipulative	16 or more	7–9	None	139
Coral Tag	Tag	16 or more	8–12	None	147
Ting, Ting, Ting	Manipulative	4	7–10	Lids	174
Tin Can Toss	Manipulative	5	8–12	Ball, can	175
NEW ZEALAND					
Open Ball	Ball	16 or more	9–12	Ball	39
Trick the Guard	Ball	2	9–12	Ball, goal	92
Beanbag Tag	Tag	5	7–12	Beanbag	96
Magic Raygun	Tag	16 or more	9–12	Sticks	128
War	Ball	16 or more	9–12	Balls	142
Balance Challenge	Manipulative	2	8–12	Cones, planks	160
Interceptor	Ball	8	9–12	Ball	181
Animals	Manipulative	16 or more	9–12	None	187
NIGERIA					
Fire on the Mountain	Run	16 or more	7–12	None	11
Lion in the Den	Run and Tag	16 or more	6–10	None	30
Hitting the Snake	Ball	4	6–8	Ball, hoop	52
Animals Have Horns	Guess	5–9	7–10	None	76
One-Legged Fight	Manipulative	16 or more	10–12	None	139
PERU					
Rabbit in the Hole	Tag	16 or more	6–8	None	4
Carbonales	Run	16 or more	8–12	None	25
Seven Sins	Ball	9–12	8–12	Ball	36
Arquitos	Ball	3	8–12	Ball	46

(continued)

Name of Game	Type	Players	Age	Equipment	Page
PERU (cont.)					
Magazine Ball	Ball	2	8–12	Ball, magazine	89
Quechibola	Ball	5	8–12	Balls	95
Columbola	Ball	6	7–10	Ball	113
Wizard	Tag	16 or more	8–12	Sticks	136
Grasshopper	Manipulative	16 or more	7–10	None	188
POLAND					
Squares	Ball	4	10–12	Ball	53
Initiator	Guessing	6–8	7–10	None	78
An Eye	Ball	6–10	8–10	Ball	115
Chocolate	Manipulative	6–14	7–12	None	118
Yo-Yo	Manipulative	16 or more	10–12	None	126
ROMANIA					
Oina	Ball	6	7–12	Ball, stick	48
The Jobs	Manipulative	16 or more	7–9	Small objects	73
Dangerous Circle	Ball	4	7–12	Hoops, ropes	106
Flying Saucers	Run	8	7–9	Hoops, rope	116
The Conductor	Guessing	16 or more	7–10	None	133
Truck and Tractor	Tag	16 or more	8–10	None	135
RUSSIA					
Gorodki	Manipulative	2–4	10–12	Sticks	78
Log Roller	Manipulative	2	9–12	Log	108
SAUDI ARABIA					
Chase in Order	Run and Tag	10–12	8–12	None	34
SCOTLAND					
Goal	Ball	3	8–12	Ball, cone	46
Leapfrog	Manipulative	16 or more	8–12	None	66
Easa Matessa	Manipulative	5–10	7–10	None	72
Throw, Catch, Run	Ball	2	8–12	Ball, box	87
Help	Tag	16 or more	7–12	Sticks	130
SINGAPORE					
Wall Refuge	Run and Tag	6–10	9–12	None	30
Yea String	Manipulative	4 or more	9–12	String	76
SOUTH AFRICA					
Running Steps	Tag	6–12	9–12	Stairs	9
Stinger	Run and Tag	16 or more	8–12	Ball	20
Hop, Skip, Jump	Ball	2	8–12	Hoops, cones	88
One-Legged Concentration	Ball	5	8–12	Ball, cones	100
Hog Ball	Ball	16 or more	8–12	Balls, hoops	148
Double Tag	Manipulative	2	8–12	Beanbags, hoops	160
Beanbag Smash	Ball	3	8–10	Ball, beanbag	167
Frog, Jump, and Slide	Manipulative	5–6	8–12	None	177

Name of Game	Type	Players	Age	Equipment	Page
SPAIN					
Crazy Circle	Tag	8–10	9–12	None	29
Gypsy Wrestling	Manipulative	16 or more	9–12	None	77
Petanca	Ball	6–14	8–12	Balls	117
SWEDEN					
Tradhok	Run	16 or more	7–12	Sticks	10
Katter	Manipulative	5	7–10	Small object	100
Bokstarsboll	Manipulative	4–5	7–9	Ball, hoops	104
Stick Hunter	Tag	16 or more	7–12	Sticks	131
Snabbmal	Ball	3	8–12	Ball	168
Bildaren	Tag	16 or more	9–12	Mat	191
SWITZERLAND					
Tail of the Rat	Run and Tag	16 or more	9–12	Recorder	34
One, Two, Three	Run and Tag	16 or more	9–12	None	34
Countries of the World	Ball	6–15	7–12	Ball	50
Snatcher	Ball	5	9–12	Ball	106
SYRIA					
Add a Movement	Run and Tag	16 or more	7–10	None	35
Countries	Ball	6–20	8–12	Ball	53
UNITED STATES					
Red Rover	Run and Tag	16 or more	7–12	None	15
Dodgeball	Ball	16 or more	8–12	Ball	40
Ula Maika	Ball	16 or more	8–12	Ball	44
Hopscotch	Manipulative	2–4	7–12	Small objects	65
Search for the Name	Manipulative	16 or more	8–12	None	72
Scoop Ball	Ball	2	9–12	Ball, bottles	92
Spell and Catch	Ball	5	8–12	Beanbags	101
Checkmate	Manipulative	7–9	7–9	Blindfold	113
Go for It	Tag	16 or more	8–12	Sticks	135
Circle Catch	Ball	2	8–12	Balls	164
Soapbox Soccer	Ball	3	9–12	Ball, cone	171
Crossover Volleyball	Ball	12–14	10–12	Ball, net	182
WALES					
Ice Cream	Run	16 or more	6–8	None	17
Roll Ball Home	Ball	3	9–12	Ball, goal	47
Rope-Skipping	Manipulative	1–20	6–12	Ropes	70
Ball Catch	Ball	2	8–12	Ball, basket	89
Surprise, Surprise	Ball	5	7–9	Ball	97
Avoid the Circle	Tag	6–8	9–12	Ball	112
ZIMBABWE					
Eagle Eats	Tag	10–12	6–8	None	16
Twenty-Five	Ball	10–12	8–12	Ball	48
Without Hands	Manipulative	16 or more	8–12	Stones	130
Double or Nothing	Ball	4	7–10	Balls, cans	104
Dragnet	Manipulative	16 or more	7–10	None	123
Give and Take	Manipulative	10–12	8–12	Stones	182

INDEX